To
Christina, Heather, and Payden

CONTENTS

  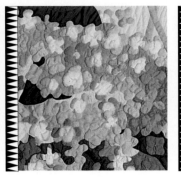 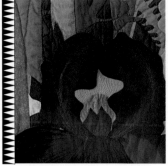

Geranium, 1993, 82" x 98". Hand-dyed fabrics in olive green, acid green, and green with a tinge of blue lend a look of realism to the leaves.

About This Book

I can't recall when Velda and I began to talk about doing a book about her work, but I remember clearly the first time I saw one of her quilts. "Iris" was the featured quilt in my guild's annual show. I had heard about Velda Newman's quilts from friends and had read an article about her in the local paper, but I was not prepared for what I saw. ❧ "Iris" was the most extraordinary quilt I had ever seen: a bold, beautiful blend of sophisticated colors and shapes. This was more than a quilt—it was a fabric painting, a work of art. I admired it from a distance, but when I tried to get a closer look, a small crowd blocked my view. I wandered the aisles until I got my chance to see "Iris" up close. The colors, the composition, the quilting—it was magnificent! ❧ I, and many other quilters in and beyond our little community, continued to enjoy Velda's quilts over the next few years. "Freedom Is Fragile" possessed a visual and emotional power rarely seen in quilts. "Nasturtium" and "Hydrangea" amazed everyone with their intricate appliqué and exquisite colors. Late in 1990, Velda and I wrote an article for *Threads* magazine, which appeared in the June/July 1992 issue and featured "California" on the cover. After that, she made "Geranium," my favorite quilt. ❧ By then, I believed that Velda and I would eventually collaborate on a book. I admired Velda's dedication to excellence and felt that her quilts deserved to be seen by a wider audience. I also thought it would be challenging—and fun—to immerse myself in her quilts and attempt to articulate her philosophy of color and design. What could be more exciting than writing a book about breathtaking quilts? By the time Velda had finished "Wings," we were ready to begin. ❧ In the process of writing this book, Velda and I have spent many hours talking about her quilts and her approach to color and design. Analyzing the quilts and explaining how color, scale, and composition combine in her designs has opened my eyes to new ways of thinking and working. And, as a hopeless perfectionist, I have been comforted by her heartfelt advice to all quilters: Take the time you need to get it right. Be willing to experiment. Never lose sight of your idea. ❧ I am "the pen" behind the words you will read in this book, but the vision is Velda's. I hope you will gain valuable insight into how she creates her extraordinary quilts.

Christine Barnes
Grass Valley, California
June 1995

A Certain Style

I invite you to look through the pages of this book and see what my quilts say to you. My approach to quilt design is similar to a painter's: I use color, composition, and scale to capture the spirit of nature, but through the medium of fabric and thread. My love of color and my affinity for nature are obvious in my quilts. The soft tints of an iris, the elegant form of foxgloves, the patterned perfection of butterfly wings—I am endlessly enchanted and inspired by the natural world. ◙ Nature's colors and patterns are the essence of my quilt designs, but scale is what makes them unique. Many classic works of art depict nature on a scale smaller than real life. A landscape places you in a relatively distant position, and even a still life may portray the subject at less than its actual size. I do just the opposite: I take life and amplify it. My geraniums, butterflies, and sunflowers are much larger than those you see in your garden. When you stand in front of one of my quilts, I hope you will feel surrounded by its vast color and sweeping shapes. Color and composition are essential elements in my designs, but the greatest emotional and aesthetic impact comes from their larger-than-life scale. ◙ Although this book is about my quilts, there is so much more that can be done. I want you to be inspired by the ideas and techniques that you see on these pages, but your quilts don't have to look anything like mine. Instead, they should be your interpretations of subjects that you love, made by your hands. Notice how I work, then look to yourself for inspiration and act on your ideas. You won't know how wonderful they are until you explore and develop them. ◙ Finally, a word of encouragement before you turn the page: Always work from your heart. It's fine to be interested in how others respond to your quilts, but you must be true to yourself. Listen to your own voice and follow your vision.

Velda Newman
Nevada City, California
June 1995

Hydrangea, 1985, 84" x 99". To capture the color and design of hydrangeas, I hand-dyed a spectrum of blues and appliquéd a multitude of tiny blossoms. A warm yellow backdrop balances the cool colors.

Color and Design

Fabric is my medium and nature is my subject, but color is my passion. Wherever I go—to my favorite nursery to pick out a flat of pansies or to the farmer's market to buy summer produce—I notice and appreciate color. I love the saturated colors of nature, and I strive for unpredictable color schemes in my quilts. I'm especially fascinated by colors used in combination. How will English bluebells look interspersed with creamy yellow freesias? What color will warm up a cool scheme of lavender-blue and deep green? Color is a powerful tool for giving expression to an idea. It is also a simple pleasure, something to freely enjoy. ❧ Color is not just the province of those in the arts. It is accessible to all of us, no matter what our interests or expertise. The key is to experience, not just see, color in every avenue of your life. Through awareness and observation, you can develop a keen color sense and begin to move away from color schemes that have lost their freshness. ❧ For most of us, design is even more mysterious and intimidating than color. Whenever people see my quilts at shows or lectures, they ask me how I come up with my ideas and how I develop them into quilt designs. Where did I get the inspiration to make a quilt based on California fruit? Why do my irises look so real? How did I create the illusion of depth and space in a tangle of nasturtiums? In short, how did I do it? ❧ Designing an original quilt is not an exact science. It's more a matter of observing and choosing, doing and changing, then doing some more. If all goes well, you get an idea, let your mind run with it, and turn it into something that pleases the eye. In reality, the design process is complex, ongoing, even annoying, and you'll take many side roads on your way to making a quilt that you love. There are no formulas for all of this, of course, but there are approaches to color and design that work for me. They can work for you too.

A Beginning

We all start somewhere, and like many contemporary quiltmakers, I began with traditional quiltmaking and evolved. It's probably accurate to say that my success was born of frustration. I've always loved fabric, and when my daughters were young, I decided to make traditional quilts using classic butterfly blocks. (Little did I know that butterflies would be back in my life, in a very big way, years later; see "Wings" on pages 90–91.) I loved choosing the fabrics and appliquéing the blocks, but when the time came to put it all together, I got bogged down. Making the blocks was fun; sewing them together was *work*. I gave the blocks to an accomplished local quilter who turned them into wonderful quilts. It was obvious that I would never become an avid traditional quilter. ❧ What seemed like the end of my quiltmaking career was really the beginning. A few years later, once I had the chance to think of things other than family, my desire to make quilts returned. In 1983, I read about a quilt contest in Santa Rosa, California. The rules seemed refreshingly relaxed: the entries could be traditional or nontraditional in both subject and technique. I didn't know any quilters at the time and just assumed that I could design an original quilt. There wasn't anyone to tell me "no." I gave myself three months to make my quilt and started right in. ◧ The result, "Cows in the Meadow" is a whimsical, folk-art farm scene. The composition called for appliqué, and I actually looked forward to putting together the pieces because nothing had to match. What a relief! And it was fun. Making "Cows" was more like painting with fabric. Once I realized that I could achieve the look I wanted using a technique I enjoyed, I was

on my way. To sweeten the experience, my quilt won a special judge's award from Jean Ray Laury. ◧ I learned several valuable lessons from making "Cows in the Meadow." First and most important, I discovered that I could design my own quilts without following someone else's pattern. Now, with a number of successful quilts behind me, I have confidence in my design ability, but then it was a big revelation. ◧ Just as important, I learned that it isn't necessary to follow rules imposed by others, or for that matter, rules I felt I should impose on myself. When I first started bleaching fabrics, I had the sneaking suspicion that I was cheating because my quilt wasn't all appliqué. That was ridiculous. Who was I cheating? I soon realized that I had to trust myself in order to go forward in my work. I

Cows in the Meadow,
1983, 68" x 72".
I created custom cow fabric by dropping bleach onto the wrong side of black velveteen. The details in the cows and the miniature farm scenes are embroidered.

needed to break the rules—or make my own rules—to develop my techniques. I was, after all, making quilts for myself. ❧ After making "Cows," I remember thinking, "I can try anything now." My mother's irises were in bloom at the time, and I was drawn to their rich colors and details. I collected photos from magazines, books, and catalogs, and made my first sketch, a composite of what I saw in the garden and in the photos. Using pictures and real irises as my guides, I gathered all-cotton fabrics in a range of natural colors. I couldn't wait to begin. ❧ At about this time, the proverbial light went on: bigger was better. Working large would allow me to appliqué complex shapes that I could never include in a smaller quilt. Executing my iris design required "thinking big." ❧ I saw other advantages to working on a large scale. I wanted to make quilts people would notice, and I knew that size alone would make a strong impression. I was also intrigued by the idea of creating one large composition that contained many small compositions, like a lot of little pictures within the big picture. And I liked the challenge of designing and making a quilt that would be interesting when seen close up or from a distance. I wanted all who saw my quilt to find something of interest, wherever they stood. ❧ With these thoughts and feelings swirling in my mind, I started and finished "Iris" (at right and on page 56) in 1985, and, to my surprise and pleasure, won First Place in Appliqué at the American Quilter's Society show in Paducah, Kentucky. "Iris" also won Best of Show and the People's Choice Award at the American International Quilt Association show in Houston. With two large quilts completed and recognized, I was eager to develop more designs inspired by the natural world I loved.

The delicate colors and elegant shapes of irises inspired me to design my first botanical quilt.

Iris, 1985, 84" x 102". Color, shape, line, and scale combine in this larger-than-life composition of flowers and ferns.

A Love of Nature, an Eye for Detail

Everyone is attracted to nature, especially to things that live and grow. Fall leaves, showy blossoms, brilliant butterflies, ripe fruit—they're all pleasing to our senses. We also relate easily to natural subjects depicted in the fine and decorative arts. ❧ I love nature, especially the intricate colors and forms of flowers, and I scrutinize the natural world with more than a passing glance. Most people don't take the time to look carefully at their surroundings. They see a tree in full bloom, and they may comment on its beauty, but they may not take in the details. ❧ I try to see it all. On walks, I keep an eye out for interesting colors and textures in flowers and other plants. Even in the car, I notice the wildflowers by the side of the road or architectural details in the city. Being observant comes naturally; it's not something I've had to teach myself. For as long as I can remember, I've enjoyed looking—really looking—at the world around me. ❧ To find inspiration in your environment, you must see both the big picture and the minutiae. I love detail; I like to observe it, and I enjoy using it in my quilts. I also like the unexpected. Once you start to see the details and surprises in nature, you'll have much more to work with in your quilt designs. I think there's a creative law at work here: Improve your observation skills, and you will grow as a designer.

Early-morning light softly bathes poppies and wildflowers. ❧ Vibrant colors and repeating shapes create a pleasing design.

Nasturtium leaves look as though they've been splashed with paint—details you can re-create with fabric, paint, and bleach.

14

Inspiration Is Everywhere

Design ideas come from different (and sometimes surprising) sources. I love books on art, especially watercolor and gardening. Needlepoint artist Kaffe Fassett's stunning books overflow with color and design ideas. Cookbooks are another wonderful source of inspiration. Many are as much picture books as collections of recipes, and good photo styling can always generate ideas, no matter what the subject. ❧ Store displays and packaging are designed to have high eye appeal, and it's smart to check them out too. After all, manufacturers are eager to make an impression on consumers, just as you hope to capture the attention of those who see your quilt. ❧ Inspiration can come from interior design, note cards, garden catalogs, gift wrap, china, seed packets—just about anything and everything with pleasing color and design. Fine and applied art from other cultures are great sources of design inspiration. Things you've collected over the years can also spark ideas. ❧ Many of my ideas come directly from nature, when I'm out in the world and on the go. In the spring, I look forward to the yellow-orange California poppies and blue-violet lupines in the Central Valley, and in the fall, I wait for favorite trees to turn.

Among my favorite things are decorative plates, marbled fabrics, baskets, and hand-painted trout.

I see color and pattern everywhere, even in a simple basket of onions.

I can spend hours at a nursery, wandering the aisles, taking in the shapes and colors. Wherever plants grow or things are gathered—even in everyday places—you'll find ideas for quilt designs. ❧ Plants aren't the only natural sources of color and design inspiration. Think about animals when you're searching for ideas. A snake's skin, the back of a turtle, the feathers on an exotic bird—you'll find a wealth of colors, textures, and patterns in the animal world. My largest quilt is based on the colors and patterns of butterfly wings.

Color Comes First

Quilters often ask me which comes first in a quilt, the color or the subject. It happens both ways, but more often than not, color is the catalyst. The design for "Hydrangea" (pages 72–73) came out of my desire to use blue, lavender-blue, and periwinkle. These are wonderful colors in the garden, and I was intrigued by the hydrangea's large leaves and delicate blossoms held up by minuscule stems. ❧ For "California" (pages 78–79), I started with deep purple for the grapes, then completed my palette with warm apricot, golden yellow, rusty pink, and green-brown. Real plants and a collection of hand-dyed red fabrics inspired me to design "Geranium" (pages 84–85). ❧ Color is the driving force behind my quilt designs, and I think it has the most immediate impact on viewers. At quilt shows, people respond quickly and easily to color, no matter what the quilt pattern. The subject may be tantalizing and the quilting impressive, but color is the "hook."

Displays of fruit, vegetables, even crabs at an open-air market are great sources of design ideas. ❧ The appealing colors and intricate shapes of flowers just beg to be translated into quilts.

I've counted at least ten colors in the bark and leaves of eucalyptus trees.

Nature's Colors

Once you raise your awareness and train your eye, you'll begin to see the astonishing range of hues in nature. I can't overemphasize the importance of getting out and seeing things. Go to your local nursery, visit an arboretum, or admire the garden down the street. Nature's glorious colors are everywhere. ❧ Flowers are my greatest source of inspiration, but I see fascinating color in natural things some people take for granted. In grammar school, didn't they tell us to color our trees green and brown? But that's just the beginning of tree colors. Wispy birch trees have papery bark that's a blend of cool gray, chalky white, and soft beige, and the leaves, depending on the time of year, range from yellow to blue-green. ❧ The trees on my mind these days are eucalyptus, which are native to Australia, but grow in large stands in coastal California. Some people think they're rather uninteresting, but I'm fascinated by their subtle colors. The bark and leaves display a variety of soft hues—copper, yellow, green, beige, taupe, cream, blue, and gray. The inner side of the peeling bark can even be a delicate pink, like the inside of a seashell. I could do an entire color study based on eucalyptus bark. I keep thinking about it, and I suspect that I will make a eucalyptus quilt someday. ❧ Plants of one color also inspire design ideas. Subtle variations in value make the difference in these compositions.

Beyond Realism

At this time in my life, I'm interested in creating quilts that are realistic, not abstract. In another five years, I may turn to abstract images, but now I want to depict things that are real. ◙ The dictionary definition of "realism" is simple: "fidelity to nature or to real life and to accurate representation without idealization." One look at my quilts and you'll see that's not what I do. Although I've come up with techniques for achieving realistic effects, my quilts are not, strictly speaking, "accurate representations." What's the difference, and why is it important? ◙ I never try to reproduce nature in my quilts. Instead, I take artistic license with my designs, exaggerating some colors and qualities for greater impact. I try to go beyond realism, to elaborate on nature, to capture the essence of a flower without attempting to replicate it. In the art world, there's a phrase for this concept. An artist refers to "keying up," or intensifying, the color in a painting. To key up a composition might mean to make some shapes more dominant than others. ◙ You can see this concept in famous works of art. Painters such as van Gogh, Cézanne, and Monet took their subjects beyond their natural shapes, textures, and colors. They modified color and form to create something that's recognizable but not literal, something we call art. ◙ Color in art, whether it's a quilt or a painting, is often dramatically different from color in nature. In "California" (pages 78–79), the purple grapes and the gold and rust pears are larger and brighter than life. I want the fruit and other natural subjects in my quilts to look like what they are—only more so. ◙ Many of nature's colors don't require elaboration, of course. It's hardly necessary to enrich a salmon pink primrose, though you might exaggerate other colors in the design. I certainly didn't need to key up the blossoms in "Geranium" (pages 84–85). But I did elaborate on the design by choosing a brilliant blue for the background. This color isn't found in the natural setting of geraniums, but it balances and amplifies the reds and greens.

Creating depth in a one-color composition is a challenge, but I'm fascinated by the possibilities.

California, 1991, 83" x 94". In the market, you'll find pears that are a bit rusty and pink, but not as rusty or pink as the one in my quilt

19

A Design Philosophy

People sometimes ask me to articulate my design philosophy. Until I began teaching, I didn't think much about why I do what I do—I tend to work intuitively. But there are approaches to design that can stimulate creativity. To help you get started and to encourage you along the way, here are a few thoughts on design:

🌿 Do it! My first and best piece of advice is to take the plunge. Design and make an original quilt, no matter how difficult it seems. Be willing to use all the paper, time, and fabric you need. Think of time spent and materials used as an investment in your art.

At a recent quilt show, a woman told me how much she enjoyed a lecture I'd given to her guild. "I was so inspired to go ahead and just do it," she said. "I've never done anything on my own before. You gave me the confidence I needed to try."

🌿 Be bold; be subtle. I love to go to a quilt show, see a sensational quilt, and think, "Look at that!" I'm even more impressed if the quilting is outstanding. I hope to get the same response to my quilts, catching the viewer's eye with bold shapes and brilliant colors, then drawing the viewer in for a closer look at the details.

"Geranium" (pages 84–85) illustrates my approach: the larger-than-life blossoms and leaves have an impact when seen from a distance. Up close, you see the fine texture and pattern created by the stipple quilting and outline quilting in the blue background. In "California" (pages 78–79), the quilt surface is filled with shapes, but there are still surprises in the quilting that you only see up close.

🌿 Know that you can. People who admire my quilts assume I possess a talent not accessible to others. I see it differently. I believe that everyone has artistic ability, some more than others, but there is raw talent in all of us. To discover and develop your innate ability, you must abandon the idea that you can't design the kinds of quilts you would like to make. You can. It just takes practice and commitment to your work.

🌿 Do your best and take your time. What if it takes you a year? When you're finished, you'll have something you can be proud of and enjoy. I'm always willing to spend the time to get it right. I just keep plodding along until I finish. I never feel that I've given too much time to a quilt.

🌿 Don't compromise. Try not to think, "Oh, this is good enough." When I design a quilt, I have a clear idea of where I'm going with it, and I don't compromise or settle for anything less than my vision. The same holds true for the quiltmaking process: I make sure I'm satisfied with what I've done before I go to the next step. If I'm putting in a lot of time on a quilt, I want to be excited about it.

🌿 Dare to be original. Many quilters like to work from an existing quilt pattern, especially for their first quilts. They cut the required templates, then choose fabrics to match a quilt or a photo they've seen. That's fine for quilts that replicate classic designs, and many beautiful quilts come out of this quiltmaking tradition. But I've long suspected that some quilters go this route because they're afraid to strike out on their own.

It's true, designing your first original quilt is scary because you have nothing to look at or to follow. But, trust me, nothing compares to the excitement of starting from scratch, without a preconceived idea of what a quilt should be. Go with what feels comfortable, what's in you. Making a quilt that's all your own is a thrilling experience.

🌿 Take risks. In my classes, I meet quilters who want to be "safe." Playing it safe is a good idea in many things you do in life, but not in quilt design. To develop your ideas, you must overcome the notion that you should start small, be cautious, or stick to what you know. Go ahead, venture out on that proverbial limb. Sometimes you'll fall, but you'll also find yourself going higher and farther as an artist.

❦ Build on your mistakes. No one is immune to making mistakes; I know I'm not. See your failures as stepping-stones to something better. Never go back. You must go forward in your work. You must.

❦ Keep trying. A lot of quilters stop short and don't go far enough in their quiltmaking. Push yourself! Don't be reluctant to keep trying new techniques until you get the effect you want. These methods are not formulas, and you can't predict the results. I'm not heartbroken if something doesn't turn out as planned. If I bleach or paint a piece of fabric and it's a disappointment, I toss it in a pile and use it for something else. That's how painters work, isn't it? They put paint on a canvas without knowing exactly how it will look. If it works, it works; if it doesn't, try something else. You can always bleach more fabric, change a color, or undo a bit of appliqué if you don't like the effect, but you must keep trying.

❦ "What if?" I first heard this question from Sharyn Craig, and it's always a good one to ask. What if you use a gradated rather than a solid-color background fabric? What will a hand-dyed fabric look like if you brush it lightly with bleach? Ask yourself what might happen if you do something a little differently than planned. And don't be afraid of the answer.

If you don't experiment with ideas as they come up, you may later have the nagging feeling that you passed up an opportunity to improve your design. Looking at your finished quilt, you may say to yourself, "I wonder if I should have..."

❦ There's always a way. I have a vivid imagination, and if I can see something in my mind's eye, I know I can find a way to do it. That often means working things out as I go. On "Hydrangea" (pages 72–73), I didn't know how I was going to appliqué all those tiny blossoms, but I knew I could. If you work with your idea, sooner or later you'll solve the technical problems. It just takes patience and a determination to do it right.

❦ Stay open and flexible. As you work, new ideas will come to you. Don't be afraid to try something other than what you originally planned. I make changes, many changes, at every stage of design and construction. A few changes are obvious and simple, but most require careful thought and considerable experimentation.

In the early stages of "Wings" (pages 90–91), I didn't know how I was going to handle the butterfly in the lower right corner. As I worked with the design and the piece evolved, I realized that I couldn't cut off the wing, that it was best to let it spill over the edge.

❦ Value your interpretation. Even though you use techniques that I use, my work is mine, and your work is yours. Don't expect your apples (page 48) to look just like mine; your study will be your vision of the design. Value it! The ideas and techniques you take from these pages can serve as a guide, but the interpretation is yours.

❦ Work for yourself. If I can leave you with one final thought on color and design, it is this: Have the courage to believe in yourself and what you're doing, and don't be afraid to go out on your own. Again and again, I see quilters who are inhibited by what others do and say. Let them make their quilts, and you make yours. Please yourself; if others like what you do, that's great, but you must work for yourself. If it appeals to you, that's what counts.

Fundamentals of Composition

I took color and design classes in college, and I know I draw on that background, even if not consciously. A quick look at a few fundamentals of composition can help you spot and solve problems in your designs.

Depth. When I make my sketch, I instinctively layer shapes to create a sense of depth. You can see this principle at work in "California" (page 78), where overlapping shapes establish a definite foreground, middle area, and background. Even in "Apple Study 4" (below), which has just a few shapes, slightly offsetting and overlapping the apples and lemons gives the illusion of depth.

Line. Diagonal lines are pleasing in any work of art because they bring energy and movement to a design. You'll find diagonal lines in all my quilts. They aren't actual lines, the kind you might draw from one corner of a page to the opposite corner, but rather the suggestion of direction created by edges that touch or slightly overlap. Two of the flower heads in "Hydrangea" (pages 72–73) join to form a loose diagonal line. The blossoms tumble down the face of "Nasturtium" (below and on pages 66–67) in a diagonal arrangement.

What happens if a composition has no diagonal movement? Imagine the apples, lemons, and leaves in "Apple Study 4" arranged in tidy horizontal or vertical rows. Even if the pieces overlapped, the effect would be static and uninteresting. When you arrange shapes in your drawing, take inspiration from nature, which is full of diagonal movement.

Harmony. When you create both unity and variety in a composition, the design appears harmonious. Color is an effective unifier; in "Hydrangea," I used two main colors, blue-violet and deep green, throughout the quilt. Similar shapes, such as the butterflies in "Wings" (pages 90–91) or the flowers in "Iris" (above right and on page 56), also unify a quilt design.

Emphasis. As a design principle, emphasis means making some elements in a design more significant than others. Size is the most obvious way to suggest emphasis; in "Wings," the large black-and-white butterfly commands attention because it occupies the greatest area. You can also achieve emphasis by letting the focus fall on certain elements of the design, such as the statue's face and upraised arm in "Freedom Is Fragile" (below and on pages 62–63).

To achieve variety, make some shapes small, others large, even when the design consists of one repeated element. "Nasturtium," for example, features one type of plant, but the flowers and leaves vary in size and shape.

Rhythm. More obvious in traditional pieced quilts than in contemporary designs, rhythm occurs when elements, such as blocks, are repeated in an organized pattern. In my botanical quilts, repeating curves and lines, such as the sword ferns in "Iris" (above) and the pears in "California" (below), establish a strong visual rhythm.

Making the Commitment

It takes a real commitment of time and energy to design large-scale quilts. People who are not quiltmakers think my quilts just happen, that I throw a little fabric on the wall and start stitching. In reality, an idea may churn in my mind for more than a year before I begin to sketch it. Even as I drift off to sleep, I think about the colors and shapes in a current or future quilt and ask myself, "What can I do to improve this idea?" ◲ I take time to study my subject and absorb its nuances. Shapes, colors, patterns; they're all in my head. I often buy plants and look at them for weeks before I

Delicate colors and simple shapes lend themselves to quilt designs.

begin to sketch. For "Hydrangea" (pages 72–73), I bought a small bush and set it on the kitchen counter where I could see it throughout the day. ❀ I also spend long hours alone, in my studio, working out the details of a design. I make a million tiny decisions in the course of designing and making a quilt. In the end, a successful quilt is well worth the effort, but it is work and it's time-consuming. That's why I have so few quilts—nine large quilts in twelve years—but I'm happy with the ones I make. ❀ Because I spend so much time designing and making each quilt, my projects tend to overlap. While I'm working on the mechanics of one quilt, I'm preparing mentally for the next one. For several years, I've wanted to make a quilt inspired by foxgloves, and I have pictures pinned to my studio wall. Even though I'm finishing the quilting on "Sunflower State" (pages 98–99) at the moment, my thoughts are often on those foxgloves and a future quilt—the composition, the colors, the fabrics, the format. Thinking about my next quilt is a great incentive to finish the one I'm working on.

Developing a Design

I enjoy every stage of quiltmaking, but developing the design is one of the most exciting. In this section, I describe the process, beginning with the sketch and finishing with a full-size drawing. As you read and look, think about how you might use these ideas and techniques in your own quilts. And remember: designing a quilt isn't a rote task; it's a fluid, creative experience that should be enjoyed.

Choosing Your Subject

When it comes to choosing a subject from nature, your options are endless, but some subjects lend themselves to my painterly approach better than others. In my classes, I suggest that students choose bold flowers or other natural things that have broad, flat shapes—and not too many of them. Primroses, though they are small, have flat, simple blossoms that are relatively easy to depict in fabric, paint,

and thread. Wisteria, on the other hand, has tiny blossoms that can translate into countless (and perhaps frustrating) hours of appliqué. In general, stay away from complex flowers, at least until you've developed your techniques.

Tools and Supplies

You'll find the design process easier and more satisfying if you work with a few helpful tools.

Graph paper. Sketch your design on ¼" graph paper. I draw on a scale of 1" to 1'—that is, a 7" x 8" drawing for a 7' x 8' quilt.

Design wall. I work on an 8' x 12' fiberboard surface made up of three 4' x 8' sheets pushed together and attached to one wall in my studio. Fiberboard is an excellent work surface for me because I move my appliqué pieces many times as I work on a design, and fiberboard is firm and easy to pin into.

Tru-Grid®. This soft pattern web made by Pellon® features a 1" grid. I use it to make full-size drawings as well as patterns for painting and appliqué.

Reducing glass. This indispensable tool is the reverse of a magnifying glass. I use it to step back and see my design as it appears from a distance. When you look through a reducing glass, color and composition problems become more obvious than when you view the design at its actual size. Quilt shops, art-supply stores, and art-supply catalogs carry reducing glasses. Inexpensive door peepholes, available at hardware stores, serve the same purpose.

Graph paper, pattern web, and a reducing glass are indispensable for designing quilts.

Sketching a Design

At the drawing stage, I have a good sense of how I'll use color in my design. Keeping those ideas in mind, I draw my quilt design on graph paper. This sketch changes as my ideas develop, but it's a place to begin. ◙ I like to fill my quilt "canvas" with interesting shapes and intricate quilting. I rough out the large shapes first because they anchor a design, then I fill in with the smaller shapes, weaving them together into a coherent whole. On some quilts, such as "Geranium" (pages 84–85), I leave fairly large areas of the background free for quilting later. ◙ I sketch from photos and living plants. I find that it takes both: photos to help with size and spatial relationships, and actual plants for the subtleties photos don't always capture. ◙ Many of the details of my designs can't be included in the initial sketch. As I'm drawing, ideas run through my mind, and I keep a list of elements I want to add when I enlarge the sketch. In "California" (pages 78–79), I decided to add more autumn colors, so I made a note to strip piece a few of the leaves. I also wanted to create dimension in the grapevines, so I wrote a reminder to tie a few of the vines

into knots before appliquéing them to the background. ◙ It's important not to rush this stage of a design. You should take time to live with your sketch and modify it, if necessary, before moving on to the full-size drawing. I pin my sketch where I can see it frequently, and as I pass by it throughout the day, ideas come to me. I never make snap decisions at this stage; I take plenty of time to think through any changes.

Making the Full-Size Drawing

Once I'm satisfied with the sketch, I enlarge it to the finished quilt size. Scaling up drawings is a tedious process, especially when you work large. To avoid this chore, I bought an overhead projector a few years ago. I take my sketch to a photocopy shop and have it made into a transparency, then I lay the transparency on the projector and back it up until the image on the wall is the correct size. Because the initial sketch is done to scale, I know exactly how large to make the full-size drawing. ◙ I pin a length of gridded pattern web to my design wall and project the image onto it. Using a permanent marker, I draw the design onto the web. ◙ Not surprisingly, going from a sketch to a full-size drawing makes a big difference in a composition. Shapes that looked fine small may need to be redrawn once I see them full size, and areas that appeared complete on the sketch may require additional shapes. Many details can't be drawn at the sketch stage; I add them to the full-size drawing, along with background elements. ◙ I think of my sketch as a guide for developing my full-size drawing. Some people are too attached to the idea of sticking with their original sketch. Just because you drew it one way doesn't mean you can't alter it. It's easy to make changes at this stage. Stay open to the possibilities, and be willing to add, take away, or move shapes as you go. ◙ As I work, I use my reducing glass to check the proportion and

Each of my quilts begins as a sketch.

placement of the pieces in the design. My studio is fairly small, considering the size of my work, so it's essential to get a feel for how a composition looks from a distance. ⬛ A few words of reassurance about this stage of quilt design: Doing a full-size drawing takes more time than you think. Ideas churn in my head continuously, and I often spend several weeks getting the drawing just the way I want it. Even if you're discouraged, stick with it. It's a mistake to move on to the next phase before you're happy with the composition. You must be excited about your design; after all, you'll be looking at it—and working with it—for a very long time. ⬛ You may also feel fragmented by the process, but I encourage you to accept and enjoy the slow and simultaneous nature of design. You can't focus only on the arrangement of the shapes, turn your attention to color, and then go back to the composition. With a little experience, you'll learn to consider all of the elements as you develop your design.

Choosing a Background Fabric

The background fabric can kill a design or bring it to life. In many of my quilts, very little of the background fabric shows, but it plays a crucial role in the design. ⬛ To audition a background fabric, I arrange small pieces of my appliqué fabrics on it, then step back and evaluate the effect. My reducing glass is helpful in this process. Does the background fabric enhance the appliqué fabrics? Do the appliqué fabrics change color when placed on the background fabric? Does the background fabric lend a sense of continuity to the design? ⬛ Sometimes I try two or three different fabrics before finding the right one. My search for the perfect background for "Hydrangea" (pages 72–73) was typical: I assembled a hydrangea flower head and laid it on each of several possible fabrics. Light green dulled the hydrangea blues, but yellow provided just the warm, light contrast this cool quilt needed. ⬛ The background fabric can be just as intense as the appliqué fabrics. For "Geranium" (pages 84–85), I chose an electric blue that pulsates next to the saturated reds and acid greens. Because the colors are equally strong, with no obvious resting place, the eye jumps across the quilt. ⬛ Lately I've been experimenting with gradated and pieced background fabrics. For a discussion of these fabrics and how I chose them, turn to "Wings" (pages 90–91) and "Sunflower State" (pages 98–99).

My full-size drawing for "Sunflower State"

27

Iris, 1985, 84" x 102". Using bleach and paint, I created my first botanical quilt.

Fabric Manipulation

When I started working on "Iris" (at left and on page 56) in early 1985, I was frustrated by the limited selection of solid-color, all-cotton fabrics. I wanted to capture the realistic colors and shapes of irises in bloom, but I didn't see how I could succeed using commercial fabrics. It was obvious that I needed to improvise. With just a few supplies, I began to develop my techniques for bleaching, painting, and inking fabrics. ❧ I experimented with bleach first and quickly discovered its potential for altering color and creating form. At the time, I felt almost guilty about bleaching fabrics—I thought the only acceptable way to create subtle, sophisticated color changes was to appliqué separate pieces of fabric. As it turned out, I wasn't breaking the rules, just becoming more aware as an artist. ❧ Today I bleach, paint, and ink many of the fabrics you see in my quilts. On the following pages, I describe my methods for manipulating color in fabric. These techniques do not yield perfect or predictable results—that's why I like them. If a piece of altered fabric looks too good, people assume it's commercial. If it's imperfect, it's immediately more interesting. So forget about perfection—you'll have more fun with your fabrics, and you'll love the custom look they lend to your work. ❧ Before you try any of these techniques, read the instructions from start to finish and look at the photos and illustrations to get a feel for the process. Then gather your materials and work through each technique, step by step, on practice fabric. Don't be afraid to ruin some of your fabric along the way—it's never a waste of time or fabric when you're trying something new.

Fabric Selection

Isn't it amazing what's happened to fabric in the past ten years? When I was making "Cows in the Meadow" (page 12) almost no hand-dyed fabric was available to quilters. Now I can order hand-dyed fabrics in the colors I want, though my source has changed several times over the years. The selection of commercial fabric just gets better too. With so many options, it's difficult to know which fabrics will best suit your designs. Following are a few guidelines to help you make wise choices:

❧ Invest in high-quality fabric. Because I put a great deal of time and energy into each of my quilts, I want the best fabric I can find. If quilters have a fault, it's their determination to spend as little as possible. There's no substitute for good fabric. My time merits good fabric, and so does yours.

❧ Allow extra fabric, especially for small, repeating shapes such as the grapes in "California" (pages 78-79) and the petals in "Hydrangea" (pages 72-73). I usually add many more of these small pieces once I start cutting and pinning them to the background fabric. And because I cut most of my small shapes freehand, I allow a little extra for mistakes.

Types of Fabric

Cotton fabrics are ideal for appliqué because they turn under and crease easily. The raw edges of blends, on the other hand, tend to slip out when folded under for appliqué. ❧ Commercial cotton fabrics now come in a wonderful array of colors, though you probably will not find every color you need for a particular design. ❧ Because of the way they are woven, jacquards display slight variations in color, an effect sometimes referred to as tone-on-tone. The longer threads in jacquards often poke out as I needle-turn the edges, but I put up with this problem because I like the look of a jacquard in a grouping of plain-weave cottons. "Geranium" (pages 84–85) and "Sunflower State" (pages 98–99) both contain jacquards. ❧ Hand-dyed cotton fabrics have a one-of-a-kind look that's perfect for original quilt designs. You can order one-color fabrics or fabrics that have been dyed two, three, or more times. Depending on the fabric and the dye used, hand-dyed cottons can appear

A selection of commercial cotton fabrics, including jacquards

A selection of hand-dyed cotton fabrics

slightly mottled and sueded, characteristics you rarely see in commercial fabrics. ◙ I use mostly solid-color fabrics because my designs depict recognizable shapes, and prints can be distracting. Solids are also best for bleaching, painting, and inking. I have a good, small collection of solids, but I try not to stock up too much. When I need a specific color, I have it dyed. ◙ As you can see from looking at my quilts, I love to use black-and-white fabrics in my designs. "Non-color" fabrics such as black and white provide visual relief from large areas of saturated color, and the designs in black-and-white prints add variety to solid-color compositions. ◙ Tricot-backed lamé is the only lamé I recommend because it frays less and is easier to work with than tissue lamé. I like the glitz of lamé, but I have my doubts about how well it will hold up over time. "Geranium" is my most recent quilt with lamé, and I probably won't use it again. I ask myself, are the color and sparkle worth the risk? The answer for me is probably not. With cotton, there's no worry—look at how long cotton quilts have been around. ◙ In "Wings" (pages 90–91), a variety of silks capture the iridescent, shimmery quality of butterfly wings. But silk is difficult to

appliqué, especially for beginners. It frays badly— you'll think it's disintegrating right before your eyes! And as you move it, it gets worse. I found a way to work around this problem on "Wings"; see pages 90–91 for details.

Bleaching

My favorite and most-used technique for creating subtle color variation in fabric is bleaching. The center flower in "Iris" (page 56) and the rusty pink pear in "California" (pages 78–79) show the dramatic effects of bleach. ◙ Bleaching is an appealing technique for a number of reasons. The materials are inexpensive, and the bleaching action is fast (too fast, if you aren't careful). From a creative perspective, bleaching is a versatile technique: you can add lifelike dimension to a shape, break up large expanses of plain color, or establish design lines for quilting. And with bleach, you create the color change exactly where you want it. Many hand-dyed fabrics have beautiful mottled areas, but to use them selectively, you must cut into your fabric. With bleach, you can work with a piece of fabric that's close to the size and shape you need.

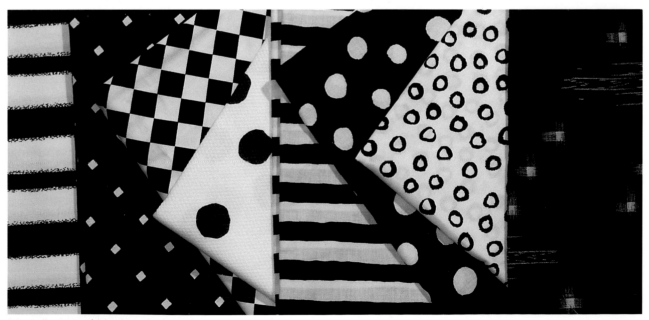

My collection of black-and-white dots, stripes, and geometric prints

To Prewash or Not?

It's not necessary to prewash most fabrics before you apply bleach. In fact, I don't recommend it. I find that it's easier to work with unwashed fabrics because their sizing makes them more stable. ◙ There's a second good reason for not prewashing fabric you plan to bleach: bleached fabric often looks different on the wrong side. I'm not sure why this happens, but I assume that the sizing affects the penetration of the bleach. Occasionally I use the wrong side of the fabric because the color change is subtler. ◙ Sizing may affect the bleaching action in other interesting ways, especially when you squirt or paint the bleach onto fabric. Sometimes the color turns lighter at the center of the bleached area, where the bleach is most concentrated, and stays darker at the outer edges. I got this result on some of the grapes in "California" (page 83). I've seen the reverse happen, too: the edges become lighter and the center remains close to the original color. ◙ Some fabrics have a heavy finish that prevents the bleach from penetrating. Prewashing these fabrics is your only option.

Tools and Supplies

To experiment with bleach on fabric, gather a few tools and supplies. You probably already have many of these materials on hand.

It takes just a few tools to achieve special effects with bleach, paint, and ink.

Bleach. Household bleach diluted with water effectively pulls the color from most fabrics. Use equal amounts of bleach and water. You can achieve a softer look if you dilute the bleach even more.

Bottles. To make batiklike lines, such as the veining in leaves, I use an inexpensive plastic squirt bottle with a snip tip. A spray bottle with a trigger handle and adjustable nozzle, similar to one you use for pressing, is useful for spattering bleach on the fabric.

Brushes. To create a feathery color change, use a flat, synthetic-bristle brush. Do not use a natural-bristle brush; the bleach will dissolve the bristles. I also use a broad utility brush to bleach larger areas of fabric.

Marking pencils and chalk. When I'm experimenting with bleach, I often cut out leaf and flower shapes freehand, but you may want to use a quilter's marking pencil or chalk to sketch the shape and interior lines.

Work area. Work outdoors on a surface that can't be damaged by spilled bleach. An outdoor table is usually adequate. Cover the table with a plastic drop cloth; also spread a drop cloth under the table.

Paper towels. Lay your fabric on a layer of newspapers covered with white paper towels. Change the paper towels before you start to work on a fresh piece of fabric. If you don't, bleach that has accumulated in the towels will transfer to your new piece of fabric, and you'll see bleaching action you hadn't planned on. These accidental effects can be wonderful, of course, but they're never a sure thing.

Caution: Bleach contains chlorine, a potentially hazardous chemical. Read the warning label on the bleach bottle very carefully.

- Never use these bleaching techniques if you have heart problems or chronic respiratory problems, such as asthma or emphysema.
- Work outdoors.
- Protect your eyes with goggles and your hands with gloves; wear a long-sleeved shirt.
- If you have any adverse reaction to the bleach, stop immediately and leave the work area.

A Word of Advice

My first tip about bleaching is don't agonize over it. Nothing is perfect in nature and you'll never achieve perfection with bleach on fabric. Remember, you're going for the suggestion of reality, not a photographic image. ◪ Every piece of fabric is different, and you never know how bleach will alter it until you try. That's the beauty of this technique. If you're disappointed in your first effort, set the fabric aside and start over. You can't really make a mistake, unless you leave the bleach on too long, but some results will please you more than others. Try to keep an open mind. I don't always know what I want when I begin to bleach a fabric; I wait to see what happens and take it from there.

Timing Is Everything

Typically, diluted bleach pulls the color from fabric in 3 to 4 minutes. I may leave bleach on longer if I want to lighten my fabric as much as possible, but I always test a corner of the fabric, timing it carefully, before I do the real thing. Generally, if the color doesn't come up in 3 to 4 minutes, you should stop the bleaching action.

What to Expect

You get very different (but equally amazing) results when you bleach hand-dyed and commercial fabrics. You can never predict how a particular fabric will respond to bleach, but I can give you an idea of the possibilities. ◪ I love hand-dyed fabrics because they come in such a wide array of rich, sophisticated colors. The greige goods (the undyed fabrics, pronounced "gray goods") for hand-dyed fabrics are usually white or cream, and that's often what you see when you leave the bleach on for the maximum safe time and pull all of the color. Leaving the bleach on for just a short time can yield a pale version of the dyed color, or you may see a related color. ◪ Commercial fabrics hold more than a few surprises. These fabrics are often dyed a base color to begin with, then overdyed or printed with the colors you see. Applying bleach uncovers the base color, and it may not be the color you expect. The base color in a green commercial fabric, for example, may be yellow or blue, and the base color in a purple fabric may be pink.

Bleaching reveals a fabric's base color.

If you're careful not to leave the bleach on too long, you can, in effect, create a two-color fabric. In "California" (page 79), the rust fabric for the far-right pear bleached to a soft pink, and the rust fabric for the pear at the upper edge bleached to a rich yellow gold.

Squirting Bleach

For your first practice piece, try creating a leaf using half-strength bleach applied with a snip-tip plastic bottle. ◎ Before you begin, prepare your work surface.

1. Choose a green cotton fabric. Using a fading pen, washable marker, or chalk, draw a simple leaf shape, including the veins. Cut out the shape, leaving a generous allowance around the edges, and lay it on the paper towels.

2. Fill your plastic bottle with an inch or so of diluted bleach. Place the tip of the bottle at a 45° angle to the fabric. Squirt a bead of bleach onto the fabric, moving the tip quickly over each line. If you linger in one spot, you'll leave a small pool of bleach on the surface. You may like the result, especially if you're trying to create a batik look.

3. Time the bleach. Once you see the color come up the way you want (3 to 4 minutes for diluted bleach), dunk the fabric in a large bowl of cool, soapy water to stop the bleaching action.

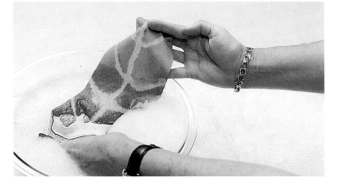

Rinse the fabric under running water.

4. Place the leaf between paper towels and pat to remove the excess water. Allow the fabric to dry.

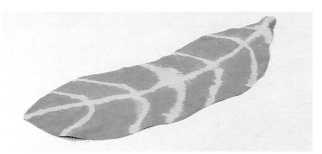

If the bleached areas are too light or still too dark, set the piece aside and try again.

Brushing Bleach

You can add depth and dimension to a flower or other shape by painting bleach directly onto fabric. The finished effect depends on how much bleach is in your brush and how you apply it. ◎ Before you begin, prepare your work surface.

1. Choose a cotton fabric in a saturated flower color, such as red. Using a marking pencil or chalk, draw the petals. Cut out the petals, leaving a generous allowance around the edges, and lay them on the paper towels.

2. Pour a small amount of diluted bleach into a glass bowl.
3. Dip your brush into the bleach and remove the excess on the edge of the bowl.
4. Beginning at the center of each petal, brush outward in quick, feathery strokes. You can achieve a gradated color change if you have just the right amount of bleach in your brush. The objective is to saturate the fabric at the center of each petal, then let your strokes fade to nearly nothing at the top.

5. Time the bleach. Once you see the color come up the way you want (3 to 4 minutes for diluted bleach), dunk the fabric in a large bowl of cool, soapy water to stop the bleaching action. Rinse the fabric.
6. Place the petals between paper towels and pat to remove the excess water, then allow the fabric to dry.

Spattering Bleach

Spattering fabric with bleach creates free-form designs. First, experiment with water in your spray bottle.

1. Turn the nozzle until the water comes out in spurts, not a spray or mist. Fill the bottle with diluted bleach.

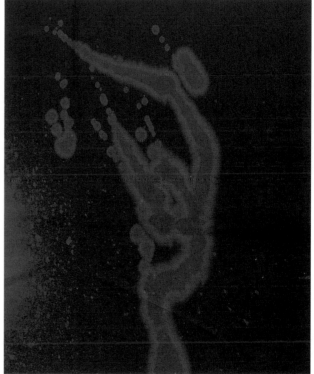

Spattering bleach creates free-form designs.

2. Prepare your work surface. Spatter the fabric with bleach as desired.
3. Use the same methods for stopping the bleaching action as described in steps 3 and 4 of "Squirting Bleach" on the facing page.

Caution: Never spray bleach in a fine mist; spraying a mist of bleach is potentially hazardous because it releases chlorine into the air. For more information, read the complete "Caution" on page 33.

Gradation Dyeing

When your quilt design calls for different values of the same color, you'll need to order hand-dyed fabrics or dye your own using the gradation-dyeing method. This process is a systematic approach to creating color. If you follow the instructions carefully, you'll achieve a beautiful series of closely related hues. ◙

I use Deka® Series L powdered dyes because they are easy to handle and readily available. They are, however, hot-water dyes, which means that the dye bath must be kept at the required temperature. You can also use fiber-reactive dyes and other cold-water dyes for gradation dyeing. Whatever dye you choose, be sure to use the required fixatives and other recommended ingredients.

Caution: Carefully follow all safety precautions listed in the dye instructions. In general, you should wear an approved dust mask when handling powdered dyes and never inhale fumes from dyes in a liquid state. Always wear gloves; it's also a good idea to protect your eyes with goggles. Keep dyes away from children. If you have any reaction to a dye, stop using it immediately.

Use only 100% cotton fabrics, such as muslin or sheeting. Prewash your fabric and keep it wet by soaking it in water overnight before you dye. Some dyes call for special wetting or prewashing agents. ◙ You will need as many dye pots as the number of gradations you want to achieve. Make sure the pots are large enough to comfortably hold the liquid and the fabric. ***Never put dye in containers that you use for food.*** ◙ How much powdered dye you use depends on the amount of fabric you're dyeing; follow the recommendation on the package.

1. To make dye concentrate, put the powdered dye in a container that comfortably holds 2 cups. (If you're using hot-water dye, be sure the container is heat resistant.) To the dye, add 1 cup of water and stir to mix. Add another cup of water to make 2 cups of concentrate.

2. Fill each dye pot with the required amount of water. Pour 1 cup of concentrate into the first dye pot. Add 1 cup of water to the remaining concentrate.

3. Pour 1 cup of the new, dilute concentrate into the second dye pot. Continue diluting and adding the concentrate to the remaining dye pots in the same manner.

4. Immerse the fabric in the dye pots and follow the manufactuter's instructions for stirring, timing, and adding other ingredients. In general, frequent stirring produces even color; leaving the fabric undisturbed creates mottled color, an effect you may like.

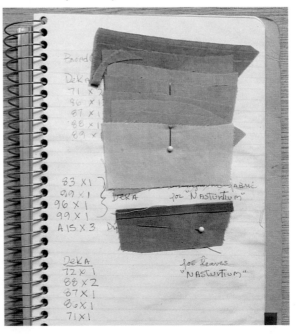

Gradation dyeing produces a subtle range of colors, from dark to light.

Painting

Practically speaking, paint is the opposite of bleach—instead of pulling color from your fabric, you apply it. Like bleach, paint offers endless opportunities for creating special effects on fabric, such as contours and highlights. Sometimes, after I've bleached a fabric, I'll use paint to emphasize an area or shape. ◙ To get a staining effect in a broad area, I dilute my paint with water. If I thin the paint enough, it doesn't stiffen the fabric after it dries. For shadows, highlights, or bits of strong color, I use the paint nearly full strength. ◙ You may find it helpful to paint watercolor or acrylic studies on paper before you paint on fabric. I sometimes do watercolor sketches to test an idea, but I often begin experimenting on my fabric. ◙ The advice I give for all phases of quiltmaking applies to painting fabric as well: be willing to experiment until you get the look you want.

Watercolor sketches are one way to experiment with color combinations and painting techniques.

Tools and Supplies

The tools and supplies you'll need to paint fabric are readily available from art-supply or paint stores, or through art-supply catalogs. A special word about fabric: Choose a fabric whose color comes closest to the predominant color of your subject. Although you'll cover parts of the fabric with paint, some (or perhaps most) of the fabric will show through. I applied several colors of paint to the apples in "Apple Study 4" (page 48), but much of the yellow-green fabric shows.

Pattern web. I use Tru-Grid to make patterns for the shapes I paint. I often draw the shapes directly onto the web, but you may prefer to draw them on paper first, then trace them onto the web.

Quilting or embroidery hoop. It's important to keep the fabric taut and to prevent it from touching your work surface. For small pieces, I stretch the fabric in the hoop, then lay the hoop flat on the counter or table so the paint doesn't run. For large shapes, staple the fabric to a wooden frame.

Fabric markers. I use a purple fading pen to draw the outline of the pattern piece onto my fabric. Some quilters have concerns about fading pens, but I've used them for years without a problem. To draw details and shadows after the paint has dried, I use Fabricmate® fabric markers in different colors.

Paint. A wide variety of acrylic and fabric paints can be found in art-supply and paint stores, and through art-supply catalogs. Some fabric stores also carry fabric paints. I started using acrylics because I had them on hand, and I thought, why not? I like Winsor Newton acrylics because they are high quality and readily available.

Mixing trays. I use an artist's white mixing tray. Trays come in plastic or metal. I prefer metal because it's easier to clean.

Brushes. You don't need many expensive brushes to paint on fabric. I use inexpensive interior house-painting brushes for making broad strokes. Save your good acrylic brushes for the details.

Hair dryer. To speed the drying process, use a hair dryer.

Painting Fabric Step by Step

For practice, try painting one or more apricots on a yellow-orange solid cotton. For the apricots shown here, you'll need yellow, orange, red, and white paints. ✿ Use the pattern on page 110, or if you prefer, draw another simple fruit shape, such as a pear. To check the proportions of your drawing, hold it up to a mirror; errors in composition are more obvious when you look at a drawing in reverse. ✿ If you don't want to paint an apricot but you're not comfortable drawing anything on your own, trace a simple shape from an illustration or photo, then enlarge it at a photocopy shop. It may take several steps to reach the size you want, depending on the enlarging capability of the machine.

1. Trace the apricot shape on page 110 onto a piece of pattern web; cut out the pattern.
2. Stretch your fabric in the hoop and trim the excess. Using your pattern, draw the apricot onto your fabric with a fading pen.

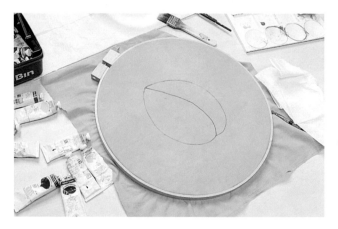

3. Squeeze small amounts of yellow and orange paint onto your mixing tray. Add a few drops of water to dilute, then stir to mix.

❧ Hint ❧
Paint is more vivid when wet, so make the color a little stronger than you want it to appear in the finished piece.

4. With the yellow-orange paint, begin painting in the crease of the apricot.

5. Following the contour of the crease, apply the paint in wide, smooth strokes. Dry the fabric with your hair dryer.

6. Squeeze a small amount of red paint onto your mixing tray and dilute it less than the yellow-orange paint. Starting again in the crease, apply the paint, blending it toward the outer edge. Dry the fabric.

7. Finish with white highlights.

Using your brown fabric marker, shade the crease for definition and outline the stem.

8. Cut out the apricot shape, leaving a ¼"-wide seam allowance around the edge.

Once you've painted several apricots or other shapes, try "Apple Study 4" (pages 48–51). Apples and lemons are simple shapes, and the contouring is fairly easy, even for beginners.

Inking

I've never seen this technique used on quilts, but I love the effect. By dotting the fabric with ink, I can visually soften the hard edges of appliqué and make a smooth visual transition from one color to another. 🔲 For consistently fine dots, I use a Koh-i-noor Rapidograph® pen with a size 0 point and permanent, waterproof Rapidograph ink. 🔲 To ink small areas on a quilt, you can use a fine-point, permanent, waterproof marker, available at quilt shops and fabric stores. But be aware that the tips on many markers will eventually wear down and your dots will gradually become larger, an effect you may or may not like. I suggest that you experiment with several pens before you choose one.

Inking How-To's

I do ink work after I appliqué but before I quilt. Sometimes I ink as I'm quilting. 🔲 Inking works best on a light fabric that adjoins a dark fabric. In "Wings" (pages 90–91), I used ink on the orange-and-white butterfly and the large black-and-white butterfly. 🔲 To create a natural, random dot pattern, I ink in circular patterns, starting close to the appliqué fold, then I fill in the blank areas. 🔲 Ink has other possibilities. I use a marker to outline small shapes, such as the stems on fruit, because I have more control with a marker than with paint. For best results, always use your marker on dry fabric. 🔲 I also use the side of my marker to shade shapes, such as the apple branch in "Apple Study 4" (page 48).

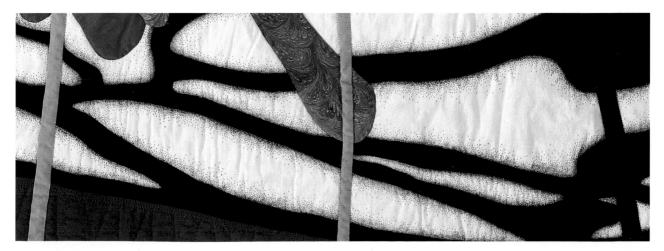

On the large black-and-white butterfly in "Wings," I concentrated the ink dots close to the black appliqué, then scattered them as I moved farther into the white silk.

Wings, 1994, 180" x 62". For this large quilt, I needed to adapt my appliqué and quilting techniques to silk fabrics.

Quilt Assembly

For me, the most anticipated and exciting moment in making any quilt is cutting the fabric and pinning up the first color. Suddenly my design takes shape, and the quilt I imagined and drew becomes real. ❧ Other parts of quilt assembly, such as appliquéing and trimming, are tedious. Quilting is also time-consuming, but it offers lots of design possibilities. I enjoy each step, whether it's mechanical or creative. They are all part of the process.

Tools and Supplies

The following list includes the tools and supplies I use to assemble my quilts. Some are absolute necessities; others are useful, though not essential.

Pattern web. I use Tru-Grid to make patterns for the appliqué pieces.

Scissors. Use high-quality sewing scissors for cutting fabric. Small embroidery scissors with sharp points are useful for trimming the appliqué layers from the back.

Pins. Glass-headed pins are adequate for all pinning.

Needles. I appliqué and quilt with a No. 10 Clover quilting needle or a high-quality English quilting needle.

Thread. I appliqué with Mettler Metrosene Plus polyester thread. I use Dual Duty Plus® cotton-wrapped polyester thread for quilting.

Batting. My choice of batting depends on the fabric I'm using and the type of quilting I plan to do. Mountain Mist Quilt-Light®, a low-loft polyester batting, works well. It may beard on dark fabrics, but it's soft and easy to hand quilt. ❧ In "Wings" (pages 90–91), I used Hobbs Heirloom Cotton, which is 80% cotton and 20% polyester. The more you work with this batting, the softer it becomes and the easier it is to hand quilt. ❧ Thermore®, a stable, lightweight batting by Hobbs, is ideal for clothing.

Markers. On light fabrics, I use a purple fading pen to mark my quilting designs; I mark dark fabrics with my Chalkoner®. The chalk stays on long enough to complete the quilting, yet it's easy to brush off once I finish.

Hoops. I use a 24" oval hoop for most of my quilting and a half-oval hoop for the edges. A hoop suits my working style better than a quilting frame because a frame takes up so much space and you must work wherever it's set up. I like to quilt in a chair, and I can work for hours if I'm comfortable.

Magnifying lamp. A round magnifying lamp on a stand is indispensable for appliquéing and quilting dark fabrics, especially at night.

A collection of tools and supplies for quilt assembly.

Making Patterns

Before cutting any of my fabrics, I study my full-size drawing to determine which pieces require patterns. I make patterns for the large shapes, such as the pears in "California" (pages 78–79), but I cut the small pieces freehand. I don't bother to make patterns for small, simple shapes, and I don't mind discarding the few that don't turn out right. ❧ To make a pattern, I lay a piece of pattern web over my full-size drawing, trace the shape, and cut it out on the line. I don't include a seam allowance at this stage—that's added when I cut the fabric piece.

Strip-pieced leaves in "California"

Pieced butterfly in "Wings"

Making Pieced Shapes

Most of the appliqué shapes in my quilts are single pieces. Occasionally I strip-piece shapes, such as a few of the autumn leaves in "California" (page 78). Strip piecing is a great way to add color, pattern, and texture to a shape or an area in a quilt. I could never have appliquéd the silk segments that comprise the golden orange, blue, and orange-and-white butterflies in "Wings" (pages 90–91), so I pieced them. By changing the direction of the grain from segment to segment, I achieved subtle variations in color and iridescence.

Cutting and Pinning

Once the patterns are made, I pin the full-size drawing to an adjacent wall for quick reference. Using chalk, I measure and mark the midpoint and a 1' grid on the background fabric, then pin it to my design board. I also mark a 1' grid on the full-size drawing. ❧ I cut and pin the large appliqué pieces to the background first. Although I have a general idea of which fabrics to use where, my choices are intuitive and subjective—I go with what pleases the eye. ❧ I pin the pattern to the appliqué fabric and cut out the piece, adding ¼" for turning under. I allow a bit more on the large pieces, up to ½", just in

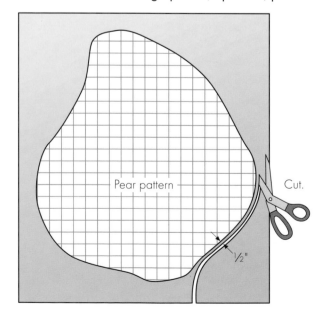

Pear pattern   Cut.

½"

case it seems short on one edge or if I want to lap one shape over another. ❂ I often cut the same shape from two different fabrics, then audition each one. I make subtle changes in some of the pieces as I cut them—a bit more contour on the outer edge, a softer curve. ❂ Even if a piece will be partially covered by others, I cut out the complete shape. For "California" (pages 78–79), I cut out the entire pear that appears in the middle of the quilt, including the lower curve. Cutting the entire shape allows me to play with the placement at the pinning stage. If I cut a shape exactly as it appears on the full-size drawing, I have no flexibility. ❂ Referring to the full-size drawing, I arrange and pin the pieces to the background, layering the pieces as I go. I pin straight into the fiberboard so I can move the pieces quickly and easily. Some fabrics have a slight nap, which makes them adhere to the background fabric without pins.

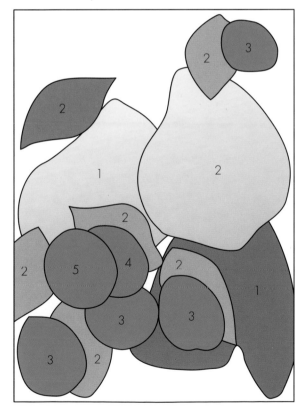

As I pin, I step back and study the impact of the colors and shapes. The reducing glass, so helpful in making the full-size drawing, is equally valuable at

this stage. I keep moving shapes until I'm satisfied with their arrangement. It's especially challenging to place the large, dominant shapes. With "California," it took me a long time to find the right place for each of the pears. ❂ It's impossible to include every shape on your full-size drawing. I improvise at this stage, filling in empty areas with small pieces. Sometimes that means adding many more of one element, such as the blossoms in "Hydrangea" (pages 72–73). I must have cut a million of those tiny pieces, and I was finding them all over the house for months. ❂ Arranging and pinning the pieces can easily take weeks, depending on the complexity of the quilt. It's important not to rush the process. You'll be looking at the quilt for a long time, and what bothers you now will bother you even more as time goes on. Be willing to stay with each step until you're satisfied. It's always worth the time and effort. ❂ When I'm happy with the arrangement, I pull out the pins partway, turn them to the side, and pin the pieces to the background fabric. I make sure the pieces are well secured before taking down the background fabric.

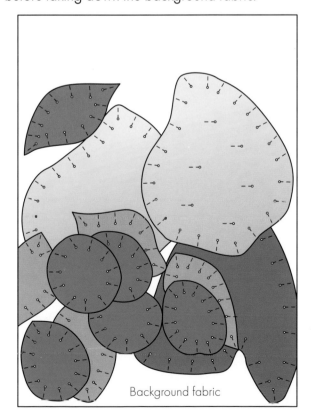

Background fabric

43

Appliquéing

Because my quilts have such a variety of shapes and sizes, I baste the pinned pieces to the background fabric before I appliqué. On large shapes, I follow the outline of the piece, being careful not to baste too close to the edge. It's not necessary to baste the interior areas of large shapes.

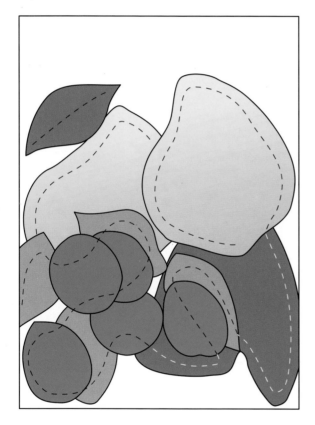

In areas with many small shapes, I baste a grid, much as I do before quilting. When I appliqué, I may need to snip some of the threads to free the edges for turning under. If necessary, I pin the piece until I finish appliquéing it. ◑ I appliqué in the same order that I pin, working from the bottom layer up. As I stitch, I catch only the layer of fabric immediately underneath. (With practice, you'll be able to feel this layer with your needle.) Catching only one layer can be tricky, but it's essential, because I trim the layers from the back

to reduce the bulk. ◑ I use the traditional needle-turn method of appliqué, turning under ⅛" to ¼". I place my stitches very close together, especially on curves.

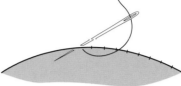

For "Wings" (pages 90–91), I needed to adapt my working method to the silk fabrics. Because the quilt is so large, I assembled each butterfly separately, then appliquéd it to the background fabric.

Trimming the Layers

It can easily take me six or seven months to appliqué a quilt top. Once I'm finished, I hang it, wrong side facing me, over a sliding glass door so the light shows through and I can see the layers. Using my small scissors, I cut away the layers from the back, beginning with the background and continuing until I get to the top shapes on the right side. I cut carefully—very carefully—to within ¼" of the appliqué stitches, which is another reason to keep my stitches close. I cut during the day only, when the light is good. This process often takes several weeks.

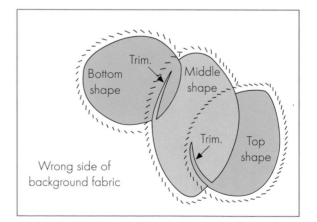

Choosing a Backing Fabric

My earlier quilts had plain backing fabrics, but the backings on more recent quilts relate to the colors and designs in the quilt top. On "Hydrangea" (pages 72–73), for example, I pieced a number of plaids that repeat the colors in the appliqué. The backing on "California" (pages 78–79) features a print of grape clusters and leaves, and "Wings" (pages 90–91) has a sunflower print that echoes the black and gold of the butterflies. On "Sunflower State" (pages 98–99), I used hand-dyed green fabrics for the backing.

Quilting

I thoroughly baste my quilt before I begin quilting. Careful basting is important because I move the quilt often, and I work on it for a very long time. I layer the backing, batting, and appliqué on the floor and pin the layers together. I baste the layers securely, spacing my stitching lines 6" apart. ◙ Quilting provides many opportunities to enhance a quilt's design. With quilting, I can outline the petals on a flower, define the veins in a leaf, or add contours to a piece of fruit. Echo quilting and stipple quilting add intriguing pattern and texture to background areas. ◙ I quilt with a variety of thread colors, depending on the effect I'm after. To add texture or dimension without breaking up the color in the fabric, I match the thread to the fabric. I use contrasting thread, especially dark thread, to create shadows or add small dots of color. ◙ I hand quilt most of my quilts because I enjoy hand quilting and I consider it a powerful design tool. Occasionally I quilt by machine, especially if the quilt is large and will be seen from afar. ◙ As I appliqué, I think about how I'll quilt. Before I make up my mind, I outline-quilt each appliqué piece ⅛" from the folded edge. Outline quilting accentuates appliqué shapes and makes them stand out in relief; it also anchors the shapes and stabilizes the quilt for further quilting. The large red petals in "Geranium" (pages 84–85) are outline quilted, as are the tiny blossoms in "Hydrangea" (pages 72–73) and the irises in "Iris" (page 56). ◙ Then I go back and do other kinds of quilting. I lay the quilt on the floor and, using my fading pen, mark an area that I know I can complete in one sitting. ◙ I usually start with contour quilting. This type of quilting follows, in a loose way, the lines of the appliqué shape. Contour quilting is effective for defining areas and creating dimension. Without contour quilting in the leaves in "Geranium" or the pears in "California" (pages 78–79), these large shapes would appear flat and uninteresting. Contour quilting is highly creative — how you contour a shape is entirely up to you.

Outline quilting in "Iris"

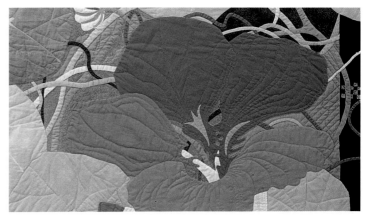

Contour quilting in "Nasturtium"

Echo quilting repeats the outline of a shape with close, evenly spaced lines of stitching, much like the ripples that occur when you toss a pebble into a pond. I use these resonating patterns to fill background areas. ❑ Stipple quilting consists of continuous, sometimes meandering, lines of stitching that never cross. I usually do this type of quilting with dark thread. I combined stipple quilting and outline quilting in the background of

"Geranium." ❑ Rice quilting, a series of random stitches, punctuates open areas with small bits of color. I used rice quilting in some of the dark background areas in "California."

Finishing the Edges

"Iris" (page 56) has a traditional border, but all of my later designs run to the edges, an effect referred to in graphic design as a "full bleed." I like the borderless look—it's as if the design continues in your mind, beyond what the eye can see. ❑ In place of a border, I use a combined edging and binding. The edging consists of one or more narrow folded strips that lie just inside the binding. This treatment is more interesting than a traditional binding, and it provides an opportunity to finish a design with unexpected color and pattern.

A double edging and a variegated binding add the finishing touch.

Echo quilting in "California"

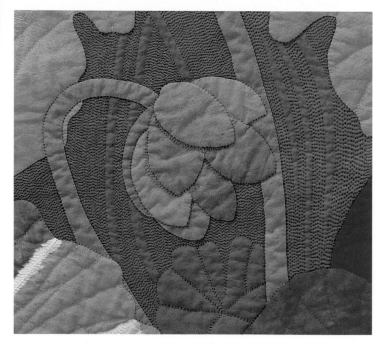

Stipple quilting in "Geranium"

I don't usually think about the edging or binding until I'm almost finished quilting; I like to let the quilt tell me what it needs in order to look complete. ❑ I often finish the edge of a quilt with fabrics that quietly repeat the quilt colors. For the edging on "California" (pages 78–79), I chose a striped fabric in autumn colors and cut the strips on the bias. I bound the edges with black. ❑ Contrasting edging and binding can really spark colors and frame a quilt. In "Hydrangea" (pages 72–73), you might expect a green binding, but I chose unpredictable, even jarring, colors—fuchsia and red for the double edging and a black-and-white stripe for the binding. I thought a striped binding and hot-colored edgings were just what this cool, flowery quilt needed.

Edging

Before I attach the binding to the quilt, I apply the edging. For a layered edging, with the bottom edging showing ¼", you must cut one strip wider than the other.

1. Cut the bottom strip 1½" wide and the top strip 1" wide. Piece the strips at a 45° angle and press the seams open. Cut each edging strip 1" longer than the corresponding quilt edge.

2. Fold each strip lengthwise, right side out, and press. Layer the strips and pin a set, with the folds pointing toward the center, to the right and left edges of the quilt top; stitch, using a ¼"-wide seam allowance. Trim the ends.

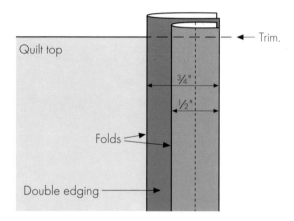

3. Pin and stitch the remaining sets of strips to the upper and lower edges, overlapping the side strips at the corners. Trim the ends.

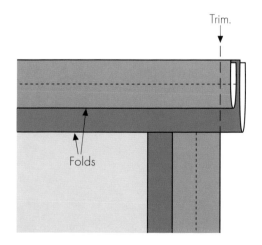

For a single edging that's ¼" wide when finished, cut 1"-wide strips. To make a wider edging, cut strips twice the desired finished width, plus ½" for two ¼"-wide seam allowances. Apply the strips as you would for double edging.

Binding

I bind the edges of my quilt with separate double-fold strips that overlap at the corners. The illustration below shows binding attached to a double edging; the procedure is the same for a single edging.

1. Cut strips 2½" wide. Piece the strips at a 45° angle and press the seams open. Cut each binding strip 2" longer than the corresponding quilt edge. Fold each binding strip in half lengthwise, wrong sides together, and press.

2. Pin a binding strip to the right and left edges of the quilt. Stitch just inside the edging stitching. Trim the ends. (For clarity, the illustration shows a shortened binding strip; it should extend beyond the upper edge of the quilt top by approximately 1".)

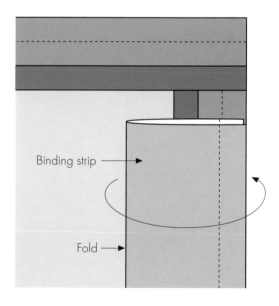

3. Turn the binding to the wrong side of the quilt and slipstitch, covering the stitching. Trim the ends.

4. Repeat with the remaining binding strips on the upper and lower edges of the quilt, turning under and slipstitching the ends.

Apple Study 4

Finished size: 35" x 24"

This small study of apples and lemons contains many of the fabric-manipulation techniques and principles of design that I use in my large quilts. Unlike my large quilts, "Apple Study 4" has both traditional and raw-edge appliqué.  If you haven't already experimented with bleach, paint, and ink, turn to "Fabric Manipulation" on pages 28–39 for guidelines and instructions. You'll probably want to paint and bleach more apples, lemons, and leaves than you need for the wall hanging. Often, your best work is not your first. I suggest that you buy several apples and look at them carefully before you begin and while you paint. You'll achieve more effective contouring and coloring if you work from the real thing. If you prefer to do very little or no painting, you can still make this study. Choose fabrics that come closest to the natural coloration of apples, lemons, and leaves. To create the illusion of form, use contour quilting in similar and contrasting threads.

Materials: 44"-wide fabrics

Note: Extra fabric is allowed for practice pieces.

¾ yd. medium green solid for apple leaves
Scraps of light yellow-green solid for lemon
    leaves
1 yd. yellow-green solid for apples and lemon
    branch
Scrap of brown print for apple branch
⅓ yd. yellow solid for lemons
⅞ yd. black-and-white dot for background
3½ yds. narrow black piping
¾ yd. backing fabric
39" x 28" piece of lightweight batting
Bleach and supplies (page 32)
Acrylic paint in green, orange, red, white,
    yellow, and brown, and supplies (page 37)
Gridded pattern web
Fading pen
Embroidery or quilting hoop
Brown, green, and gray fabric markers

Cutting

Enlarge the pattern on page 111 and use the gridded web to make patterns for the pieces. When cutting out the fabric pieces, be sure to note which ones require an allowance for turning under and which do not. *Do not cut out the apples or the lemons until after you have painted them.*

From the medium green solid, cut:
    Leaves 1–5*
From the light yellow-green solid, cut:
    Leaves 6–8*
From the yellow-green solid, cut:
    Lemon branch
From the brown print scrap, cut:
    Apple branch
From the black-and-white dot, cut:
    1 piece, 39" x 28", for background

* Allow a ¼"-wide seam allowance when you cut Leaves
    4–6; cut all other pieces on the pattern lines.

Bleaching and Painting the Leaves

1. Following the general instructions for "Bleaching" on pages 31–35 and referring to the photo on page 48, squirt bleach onto Leaves 1–3 to create veining.

2. Following the general instructions for "Painting" on pages 37–39 and referring to the photo, paint Leaves 1–4 with dilute green paint. To create the shadows in Leaf 2, use nearly full-strength green paint.

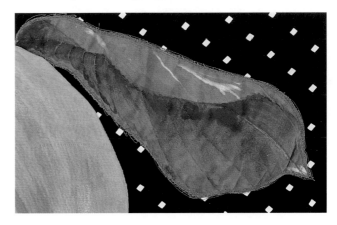

Painting the Apples and Lemons

1. Stretch a piece of the yellow-green fabric in your hoop. Using your pattern, draw Apple 3 onto the fabric with your fading pen.

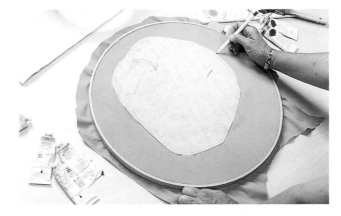

2. Following the general instructions for "Painting" and referring to the photo, paint the apple. Start at the stem end, on the shoulder of the apple. Using dilute orange paint, make wide strokes that follow the natural contours of the apple. Let the paint dry, or speed up the

process with a hair dryer. Repeat with dilute red paint. Where you want more intense color, use stronger paint.

3. Finish with white and yellow highlights. Dry the paint.

4. Using the brown, black, and gray fabric markers, outline and shade the apple stem.

5. Using the green fabric marker, speckle the apple.

6. Paint Apples 1 and 2, varying the coloration and details as shown in the photo. Use the brown fabric marker to draw the details on the blossom ends.
7. Paint Lemons 1 and 2 on the yellow fabric in the same manner, using dilute green paint on one and dilute brown paint on the other.
8. Cut out the apples and lemons, leaving a ¼"-wide seam allowance.

Appliquéing the Pieces

1. Referring to the photo and the diagram, pin the pieces to the background fabric; baste.

2. Appliqué the lemons, apples, and Leaves 4–6 using the traditional needle-turn method (page 44).
3. Machine appliqué the raw edges of the remaining leaves and the branches. I stitch back and forth many times to build up layers of stitching at the edges.

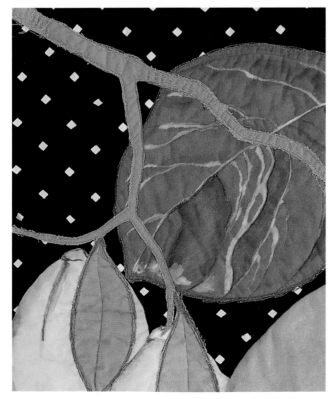

4. Using the gray fabric marker, shade the apple branch.

Finishing

1. Layer the appliquéd piece and the batting; baste.
2. Machine outline-quilt the apples, lemons, leaves, and branches.
3. Trim the piece to 36" x 25".
4. Machine baste the piping to the right side of the piece at the outer edges, rounding the corners and overlapping the ends.

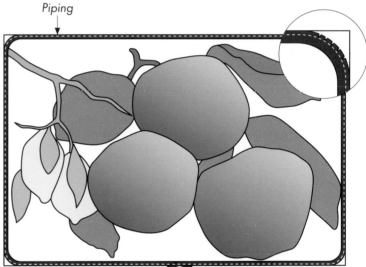

5. To make a "pillowcase" lining, place the quilted piece and the backing right sides together; pin the edges. Stitch around the edges, just inside the piping stitching, leaving a 6" opening for turning. Trim the batting, backing, and corners.
6. Turn the piece right side out and slipstitch the opening closed.
7. Add a hanging sleeve, if desired.

Gallery

Music-Making Angel

The inspiration for this quilt came from a postcard I purchased at *The Vatican Collection,* an art exhibit in San Francisco. The painting is by Italian artist Mellozzo da Forli (1438–94). I fell in love with the angel's sweet face, and I thought the painting had an ethereal quality that would translate beautifully into fabric. ◙ In the original, the angel's dress is faded, an effect I re-created by bleaching rust fabric to a soft peach. I bleached a medium gray fabric to achieve the dappled, almost translucent color in the wings. ◙ Getting expression on the angel's face was a challenge. I wanted to do more quilting, but I was afraid that extra stitching would make the face appear wrinkled, hardly the effect you want to see on a timeless angel. ◙ The slightly mottled blue background may look hand dyed, but it's a commercial fabric. For the halo, I appliquéd voile to the background and tied the layers with metallic thread. ◙ A pink and purple double edging and a taupe binding finish the edges.

Music Making Angel, 1986, 54" x 40". *A fifteenth-century portrait of an angel inspired this painterly quilt.*

I used reverse appliqué to suggest highlights, shadows, and curls in the hair.

Pieces of white voile appliquéd to a gray foundation create the impression of folds in the lower sleeves.

Iris

"Iris" was an important transition piece for me. At the time, I knew I was breaking with tradition by working on such a large scale. And manipulating fabrics with bleach and paint was certainly not the norm. "Iris," however, also contained many traditional elements, such as a relatively narrow depth of field and a wide border. If I were making this quilt today, I would probably eliminate the border and run the design to the edges. I might also pull some of the flowers forward to enhance the sense of depth. ◈ But then, I was just beginning to develop my design ideas and quiltmaking techniques—it was all uncharted territory. I built my composition around the central maroon iris, parts of which I bleached to a vibrant red. Working from the center out, I cut and pinned the flowers, foliage, and sword ferns until the arrangement pleased me. It all seemed so natural—the quilt told me along the way what it needed. ◈ When I finished the appliqué, it reminded me of a painting, so I framed the quilt with a wide maroon border. As an accent, I added narrow inner borders, one red and one orange, much like the matting on a framed picture. ◈ Then it was time to quilt. Up until that point, I thought cross-hatching and filler designs were "required quilting." But "Iris" was different from anything I'd ever done, and for the first time, I let the quilt suggest the quilting design. Much of the pale green background is contour quilted. I outline-quilted each appliquéd piece, then emphasized the shapes with echo quilting. I continued the fern and leaf quilting designs into the border. ◈ "Iris" has been widely exhibited and has taken many prizes, including Best of Show from the American International Quilt Association and First Place in Appliqué from the American Quilter's Society, both in 1985. In 1986, the AQS printed a poster of "Iris," the first in a series of posters of prize-winning quilts. "Iris" is also depicted in a stained glass window at the American Quilter's Society's museum, which opened in Paducah, Kentucky, in 1991.

Iris, 1985, 84" x 102". Irises blooming in my mother's garden sparked the idea for my first larger-than-life botanical quilt. From the collection of the Southeast Psychiatric Hospital, Athens, Ohio.

I appliquéd pieces of off-white voile to the base of the buds for a realistic effect. Folding a few leaves forward and leaving the folds unstitched creates dimension. The sword ferns add feathery texture to the composition.

A touch of orange acrylic paint on the peach iris gives it definition. All the flowers, leaves, and ferns are outline quilted.

Spraying bleach onto a navy blue fabric revealed a base color that was perfect for a deep purple iris. Stipple quilting behind the appliqué lends texture.

I sprayed and dribbled bleach onto the irises and the leaves to create mottled color.
Bits of bright yellow and royal blue enliven the design.

Freedom Is Fragile

I made this quilt for the Statue of Liberty Centennial competition sponsored by 3M in 1986. I had several goals in mind when I began to work on the design. I wanted my quilt to be graphic, to stop people in their tracks. I also wanted to say something about the nature of freedom. ◈ My first concern was how to depict the statue. For me, the most impressive part is her solemn expression and upraised arm; together they symbolize freedom's strength and resolve. To convey these intangible qualities, I came in close on the face and made it the focal point of the composition. Wherever you stand when you look at this quilt, your eye is drawn to the powerful expression. ◈ The statue dissolves into fragmented triangles in the lower half of the quilt, reminding us that freedom is fragile. If we don't protect our liberties, freedom will disintegrate. Most of the triangles are pieced; those that touch the statue and the flag are appliquéd. ◈ The flag flying behind adds a soft sense of motion to the design and frames the face and crown. To represent the states, I appliquéd or quilted fifty stars across the quilt. The narrow turquoise inner border hints at the statue's oxidized-copper color; the narrow red border symbolizes the blood spilled for our country. ◈ I'm very fond of this quilt. I like its simplicity and clarity. It didn't win the competition, but it has been well received ever since.

Freedom is Fragile, 1986, 72" x 72". I combined appliqué, piecing, and extensive quilting to illustrate the complex nature of freedom. The real statue is oxidized-green copper, but I chose to use the colors of the flag.

Stipple quilting in the crown adds texture and detail to the center of the quilt.

Narrow strips of gray appliquéd to the arm create the impression of folds in the gown; quilting accentuates the contours.

Nasturtium

Almost every spring, I scatter a packet of nasturtium seeds in my garden. They're such simple flowers, easy to grow and a pleasure to look at. At some point—I don't recall exactly when—it occurred to me that these brilliant blossoms, yellow-green leaves, and twisting stems would be wonderful depicted in a quilt. It wasn't long before I was at work on the design for "Nasturtium." ◙ The saturated red and red-orange fabrics are commercial. Contour quilting gives the sprawling blossoms form. For lifelike detail, I appliquéd bits of peach fabric to the throat area on some of the blossoms. ◙ I dyed my own background fabrics because I couldn't find just the right shades of gray or charcoal brown. I also dyed a series of yellow- and gray-greens using the gradation dyeing process (page 36). ◙ When I began to arrange the pieces on my background fabric, it became obvious that the design needed something more. I added leaves and stems, layering and intermingling the shapes until the quilt overflowed with color, line, and form. ◙ The pieced, checkered border introduces a small geometric pattern to a quilt design full of sweeping curves. A gradated periwinkle edging provides a complementary accent. ◙ "Nasturtium" took First Place in Master Appliqué from the American Quilter's Society, and First Place in Appliqué and the Judge's Choice Award from the American International Quilt Association, all in 1987. It appeared in the International Garden and Greenery Exposition in Osaka, Japan, in 1990. The exhibit traveled through Europe and the United States for two years.

Nasturtium, 1987, 96" x 90". *I wanted to portray a riot of blossoms tumbling down a garden wall with stems turning every which way, just as they do in real life.*

For the opening buds, I appliquéd pieces of pale yellow chintz, then contour-quilted the shapes in matching thread. Lots of wiggly quilting lines in the background echo the twisting pattern of the vines.

I brushed bleach on the petals in one flower to suggest natural fading.

Bleach squirted onto the leaves creates lifelike veining and irregular color. Contour quilting breaks up the large shapes and adds dimension.

For texture, I stipple quilted areas of the background using dark green thread.

Hydrangea

"Hydrangea" illustrates how quickly my approach to design and construction evolved. With this quilt, traditional borders disappeared forever, and my appliqué and quilting became more intricate. Instead of a straight-on "picture" perspective, I took a bird's-eye view of my subject, as though the viewer is looking into the middle of a blooming hydrangea bush. Flowers drip from the upper edge and "grow" from the lower edge of the quilt. The design bleeds, creating an expansive, you-are-there feeling. ◆ Designing and making this quilt presented several practical and creative problems. Not surprisingly, I couldn't find commercial fabrics in the right blues and lavender-blues. To get the range of colors I needed, I mixed blue and purple dyes and made eight or ten dye runs using the gradation dyeing process. I also dyed the lighter greens. The periwinkle in the lower right corner and the dark greens are commercial fabrics. ◆ Then I faced the challenge of interpreting these complex, delicate flowers in fabric—and finishing the quilt in this century! Each blossom is one appliqué piece, like a clover joined in the middle, but from a distance the eye sees four individual petals. ◆ I used a variety of quilting techniques across the surface: dark green stipple quilting in the yellow background, green contour quilting in the leaves, and cream and blue outline quilting around the petals. ◆ "Hydrangea" has won a number of awards, including First Place in Professional Appliqué from the American Quilter's Society, and Second Place in the Art Quilt category from the American International Quilt Association, both in 1989. It was also a part of the AIQA's invitational exhibit that traveled to Odense, Denmark, in 1990.

Hydrangea, 1989, 84" x 99". *Graceful hydrangeas spill across the quilt surface in a display of cool color and delicate form. From the collection of John M. Walsh III.*

72

To capture the essence of hydrangea blossoms, I simplified their shapes and used a spectrum of blues.

In real life, hydrangea blossoms fade in the center as they age. To re-create this natural coloration, I bleached the centers of some of the blossoms to almost white.

I took a tiny tuck and made a cross-stitch in the center of each blossom to give it dimension.

Bleach squirted onto the dark green leaves creates realistic veining. Outline and contour quilting give the leaves shape.

California

I grew up in a rich agricultural area of coastal California, near Santa Barbara, and you can see the influence of that environment in my work. This quilt brings to mind the warm summer days, vast orchards, and bountiful harvests that were an important part of my childhood. ❧ For some time, I had wanted to make a quilt based on fruit. I envisioned vibrant shades of purple, yellow, green, and brown. A composition of pears, grapes, and apricots seemed like a wonderful way to use these rich colors together. ❧ I spent a long time on the sketch and the full-size drawing for this quilt, arranging and rearranging the pieces until I achieved a balance between the large and small shapes. The purple grapes were my starting point; all the other shapes followed. ❧ This quilt contains both hand-dyed and commercial fabrics. The green-brown leaf fabric is hand-dyed; the purple fabrics for the grapes and yellow fabrics for the pears are commercial. I bleached many of my fabrics to achieve a more realistic look. ❧ "California" features every kind of quilting—outline quilting around the appliqué shapes, contour quilting on the pears and the leaves, echo quilting behind the grapes, and stipple quilting in the background. I quilted with black, rust, green, and yellow thread. Some of the thread colors match the fabrics, while others contrast. ❧ "California" won First Place in Innovative Appliqué and Best of Show from the American International Quilt Association in 1991. It appeared in *Visions, The Art of the Quilt* in San Diego, and Expo Europa in Holland, both in 1992. It was featured on the cover of the July/August 1992 *Threads* magazine.

California, 1991, 83" x 94". *The memory of the colors, tastes, and textures of summer inspired this tribute to the Golden State.*

Using a brush, I flicked green paint onto a yellow pear to suggest natural speckles.
I painted the apricots using dilute acrylic paint, then inked the details.

Bleach and contour quilting give this pear form.

For dimension, I tied some of the grapevine tubes into knots and left a few of the long edges free. When I first saw the metal bug now perched on a vine, I knew it belonged in my quilt.

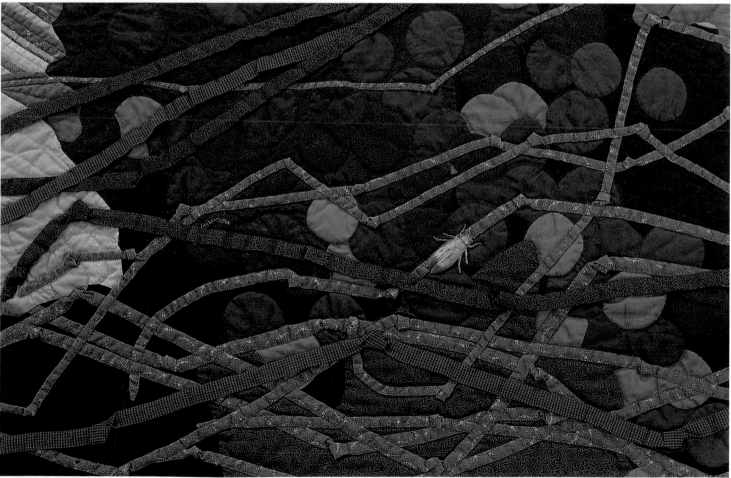

Bleach squirted onto this hand-dyed fabric revealed a peachy beige; stipple quilting brings out the leaf form.

Drops of bleach on the solid-color grapes produced soft, red-violet highlights. On the cotton lamé, only the cotton fibers bleached; on the darkest purple print, the color changed, but the black remained.

Stipple quilting and echo quilting surround the grapes, making them advance visually.

Geranium

Color comes first in many of my quilt designs, and it was certainly the case with "Geranium." At the time, I had twelve or fifteen different hand-dyed red fabrics that I was eager to use in a quilt. I thought acid green and electric blue would be powerful with the brilliant reds, and geraniums seemed a fitting subject. Perhaps a pot of them blooming on my porch triggered the idea. ◈ With every one of my quilts, I want to involve viewers in the design and envelop them in color and form. To some extent, I do this through scale. If the shapes loom large, as the geraniums do here, you naturally feel close to them. ◈ More important is the viewer's place in relation to the elements in the composition, a concept known as "point of view." In "Geranium," an eye-level view puts you face-to-face with the flowers and leaves. Layered shapes contribute to the illusion of depth, drawing you into the imaginary space. ◈ Realistic effects enhance this sense of involvement. The geraniums derive their striking form and definition from many closely related shades. The leaves also display a range of similar hues, from yellow-green to olive, even a green with a touch of blue. ◈ I left most of the blue background plain, except for the quilting. A bit of strip piecing lends variety to the background. A geometric border of black and white bias rectangles provides visual relief. ◈ "Geranium" won First in Professional Appliqué from the American Quilter's Society. In 1994, it appeared in an exhibit at the Textilmuseum Max Berk in Heidelberg, Germany, in conjunction with the American International Quilt Association Quilt Expo exhibit.

Geranium, 1993, 82" x 98". The flowers depicted are actually pelargoniums, commonly referred to as geraniums. Their rounded, variegated leaves and showy flower clusters make them an ideal subject for an art quilt.

To give the bleached area of the leaves more definition, I outline-quilted and contour-quilted them with cream thread.

Using matching blue thread, I outline-quilted the background with leaf and stem designs. Between the motifs, I created negative space by stipple quilting in black thread.

I used a fabric marker and contrasting thread to add subtle shadows to many of the shapes.

Ink spattered onto the red blossoms creates subtle texture and shadows. The shapes are outline and contour quilted.

Wings

Butterfly collecting was a favorite summertime activity when I was a child, although I wouldn't dream of doing it now. I loved looking at the intricate designs and iridescent colors in butterfly wings. They were perfection, and I was enthralled. ❂ In 1994 I was invited, along with seven other artists, to exhibit three pieces of my work in a three-month show at the Ohio Designer Craftsman Museum. I had already finished my sketch for "Wings"; the invitation was the catalyst for completing the quilt. ❂ The butterflies in this quilt are all real; that is, they are true to life in color and scale. I pored over books, looking for butterflies that would translate well into fabric. I tried to come as close as possible to the natural coloration and patterning of their wings. It was important to get every detail right. ❂ In my original sketch, I left the background plain because I didn't want anything to compete with the butterflies.

When I made my full-size drawing, I saw that the design needed a visual reference. Adding the narrow reeds helped to put the butterflies in perspective. ❂ The background consists of two lengths of gradated, hand-dyed fabric that are seamed horizontally. I chose gradated fabric because I wanted to vary the background color from butterfly to butterfly. I also felt that a subtle change in the background color would enhance the sense of spaciousness. ❂ There was never any question in my mind about which fabric to use for the wings. Silk has the luminous, iridescent qualities I associate with butterflies. I realized early on, however, that I could not successfully appliqué intricate shapes cut from silk. ❂ To solve this dilemma, I developed a variation on reverse appliqué. For the largest butterfly, I began with pieces of black cotton and white silk of the

Wings, 1994, 180" x 62". My "butterfly collection" consists of eight butterflies from around the world. The black-and-white butterfly is seven feet wide; some people don't realize that it's only one butterfly until they step back.

same size. I cut the vein structure from the black cotton, leaving ⅛" on the edges for turning under. Then I laid the black cut-out piece on the white silk and appliquéd all but the outer edges. Finally, I trimmed the white and appliquéd the entire butterfly to the background fabric. ❧ I had never done machine quilting before, and a 15' quilt was probably not the best piece to learn on, but I needed to stabilize the large shapes. I outline-quilted the butterflies but left the interior areas unquilted. In the background, I hand quilted patterns that you can only see up close. ❧ In addition to the exhibit in Ohio, "Wings" appeared in the 1995 Allegre Retreat Quilt Show, also an invitational, in Santa Fe.

I combined a hand-marbled silk and a silk charmeuse in this Indonesian butterfly. The light areas in the marbled silk were distracting, so I darkened them with a blue fabric marker. I painted the body with acrylics and embroidered it with metallic thread.

To soften the contrast between the orange and white sections of this butterfly, which is native to Malaysia, I dotted the silks with ink. I also inked the body. ❧ The black-and-white dotted butterfly in the background features a commercial fabric and an imported batik. Where I joined the segments, I inked the white dots to make the seams recede and create the illusion of veining.

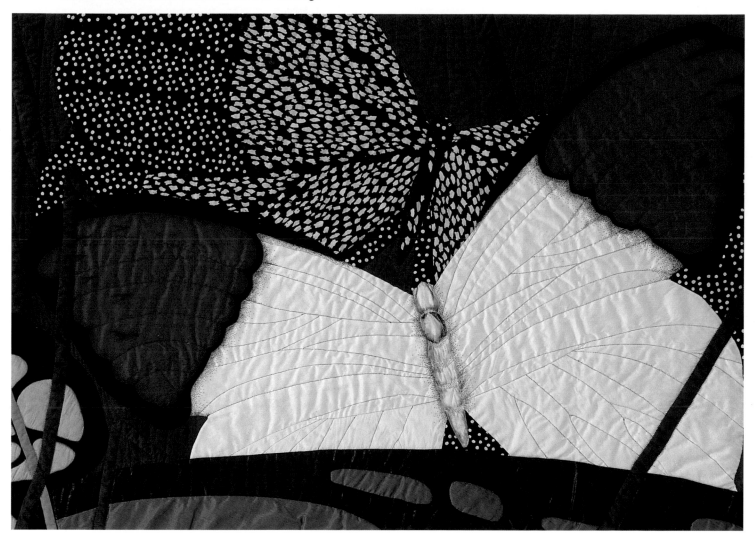

The gold segments of this Indian butterfly are slubbed silk. The body is painted with acrylics and highlighted with glitter paint. ❧ The body of the dark green butterfly, native to Central America and Brazil, appears beaded, but it's actually embroidered with metallic thread.

A small chartreuse butterfly from Malaysia complements the purple background and adds a spot of bright color.

A golden orange gulf fritillary butterfly spills over the lower
edge of the quilt. The body is painted and stipple quilted.

I outline-quilted the reeds, then quilted random designs in the background to echo the slender shapes. Stipple quilting adds texture.

Sunflower State

I broke one of my rules on this quilt. I generally like to gather all of the fabrics for the appliqué and the background before I begin cutting and arranging the pieces on my design wall. I may substitute fabrics as I go, but I start with the ones I want. On this quilt, things happened a little differently. ❂ The once-lowly sunflower now decorates many surfaces—chair cushions, dinnerware, and fire screens, to name just a few examples. Blue or periwinkle is a common background color. It's a pleasing combination, but I wanted to go a different route. ❂ In my mind's eye, I saw bright yellow sunflowers set against a backdrop of brilliant salmon pink. Yellow and pink is not a common color combination in art, but it's certainly natural. Visit a

nursery or look through a gardening catalog and you'll see many bright pink flowers with yellow centers. ⬛ With this scheme in mind, I ordered a batch of hand-dyed yellow and green fabrics for the flowers and leaves. For the background fabric, I turned to my collection of solids, but none of my pink fabrics worked. One was too dull for the brilliant yellow, and another made the yellow appear green. I also experimented with

Sunflower State, *1995, 120" x 70". Sun-drenched colors and lively shapes combine in this interpretation of Kansas's signature flower. I made each flower head different because no two sunflowers are alike.*

leftover pieces of the purple and magenta gradated fabrics from "Wings" (pages 90–91). They were powerful in combination with the yellows, but I still wasn't satisfied.  I went back to my stash and pulled out a piece of variegated, hand-dyed fabric in saturated red, yellow, pink, blue, and green. I thought this piece might be interesting with the black-and-white border, and I liked the balance between the hot and cool colors. The fabric also seemed strong enough to carry the visual weight of the large flower centers. I cut and pieced the background fabric, but it wasn't long enough. Adding small sections of a black-and-white dot

gave me the necessary length. I like the effect of the dot running through the background; it breaks up the color and gives the eye a place to rest. To prevent distortion of the flower heads, I quilted them before appliquéing them to the background. I kept my stitching very close to suggest the visual pattern created by sunflower seeds. I used a few commercial fabrics in "Sunflower State." A buttery yellow jacquard and pale yellow chintz are commercial; so are the black-and-white fabrics and the red star print (used wrong side out).

I took my inspiration from this black-and-white drawing by my daughter Heather. A sunflower design had been in the back of my mind for some time, and I liked her drawing so much that I decided to make a quilt.

Using green acrylic paint, I reworked hand-dyed fabric to create the illusion of dimension in the flower head. The petals are outline quilted. ❧ White piqué and a black solid combine in the wide geometric border. Circular quilting echoes the round flower forms.

To create near-perfect spiral quilting, I quilted a circle about midway between the center and outer edge, then worked inward, following my previous stitching. Then I returned to my starting point and quilted outward, in the opposite direction. Cross-stitches in hand-dyed, variegated perle cotton add bits of color to the background.

On this flower head, I varied the paint and the quilting design. Bleach and contour quilting define a leaf shape.

Wearable Art

Flamingo

In 1992, I was asked to make a garment for a conference of the International Federation of University Women at Stanford University. I was in the mood for something bright and sunny, and there happened to be a wonderful selection of Hawaiian and tropical print fabrics available at the time. To balance the bright colors and stylized patterns, I added a black-and-white dot. ⬢ I created the narrow horizontal wedges on the right front by piecing a series of bias rectangles. The wedges continue over the shoulder and down the back. Repeating the wedges at the cuffs unifies the design. ⬢ The strip-pieced left front, sleeve, and back serve as a bright backdrop for four pink flamingos. The light yellow in the strip piecing is a bit of a surprise among the saturated pinks and turquoise blues, but I like the visual relief it provides. ⬢ Fused-glass buttons are the finishing touch on the front band. Allover beading intensifies the colors in the prints.

Flamingo, 1992. Strip piecing, appliqué, beads, and rhinestones combine in this fanciful jacket design.

Tricot-backed lamé flamingos strike a casual pose on the jacket back. The beaks and legs (tied in knots) are made of black chintz. For the eyes, I glued black rhinestones to buttons. I also glued rhinestones to the polka dots in the black-and-white fabric. I machine appliquéd the raw edges of the flower clusters using metallic thread. Glittery fabric paint adds sparkle.

A narrow pieced band of blue, orange, and green adds color to the back of the sleeve and interrupts the chevron pattern.

Checkers, *1991. The lines in this jacket are all straight, but varying the direction brings energy and movement to the design.*

Checkers

When I first saw these hand-dyed blue and orange fabrics together, I thought they were wonderful. I decided to piece them in a simple checkerboard pattern. For contrast (and visual relief from the saturated colors), I added a commercial black-and-white stripe to the scheme. ◐ The checkerboard on the left front runs at an angle, creating a strong diagonal line. Where I joined sections of piecing, I inserted narrow strips of acid-green fabric into the seams. ◐ The chevron pattern on the left sleeve is the result of cutting and piecing the black-and-white stripe fabric on the bias. ◐ I machine-quilted random patterns on the cuffs, waistband, and collar. Black jet buttons finish the front.

I took an extra stitch at each end of each bead, then left the thread tails.

All Buttoned Up

This jacket, made for the American Quilter's Society fashion show in 1993, combines black and white in a positive-negative, interlocking design. To create the exaggerated sawtooth design, I pieced narrow bias rectangles. A dolman-sleeve jacket pattern was perfect for my design because it allowed the pieced fabric to run uninterrupted across the front and back. ❧ I wanted to embellish the jacket with buttons from my collection of black jet buttons, but it was difficult to decide which ones to use. Then I thought to myself, "I'm going to put them all on." I stitched on hundreds of buttons—old buttons, new buttons, Fimo buttons, even plastic rings. ❧ To establish visual boundaries for the wedges, I repeated the black dot fabric below the piecing and on the collar. I used black cotton ribbing at the waist and cuffs because I thought, enough is enough.

All Buttoned Up, 1993. *The color combination may be classic, but this wearable display of buttons is definitely nontraditional.*

Old and new buttons keep company with Roman shade rings.

Anchors

Making a piece of clothing is a nice break from working on a large quilt. I enjoy having a project that I can design and complete in a relatively short time. I made this jacket for the 1989 American Quilter's Society fashion show in Paducah, Kentucky. ✎ An unstructured bomber-style jacket is ideal for wearable art because the pieces are simple and the lines are flattering. Silk seemed the perfect fabric for this design—shimmery silk charmeuse for the jacket pieces, silk broadcloth for the ropes and anchor, and raw silk for the stars.

Anchors, 1989. The ropes consist of bias tubes appliquéd to the jacket front, back, and sleeves. The gold stars are appliquéd and outline quilted.

Bugle beads, seed beads, and gold anchor buttons decorate the front placket and neckline.

A single anchor hangs from a rope on the jacket back. The supple silk fabric and soft gathers at the waist and cuffs enhance the watery effect.

Africa

The design for this jacket began with the beige hand-batiked leaf fabric, a gift from a friend. It's actually a home decorating fabric, but I thought it would be striking in a garment. The black-and-gold stripe and the floral fabrics are from Africa. I bought them in San Francisco, thinking they would be interesting used in combination with the leaf batik. ◈ To add color to the composition, I appliquéd strips of a periwinkle print and a black-and-white stripe. The angular arrangement makes a nice contrast to the curvilinear designs in the main fabrics. I used narrower strips of periwinkle and black-and-white to trim the placket, waistband, and cuffs. ◈ Random circles introduce another geometric element to the design. As an accent, I made some of the circles red.

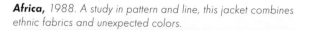

Africa, 1988. A study in pattern and line, this jacket combines ethnic fabrics and unexpected colors.

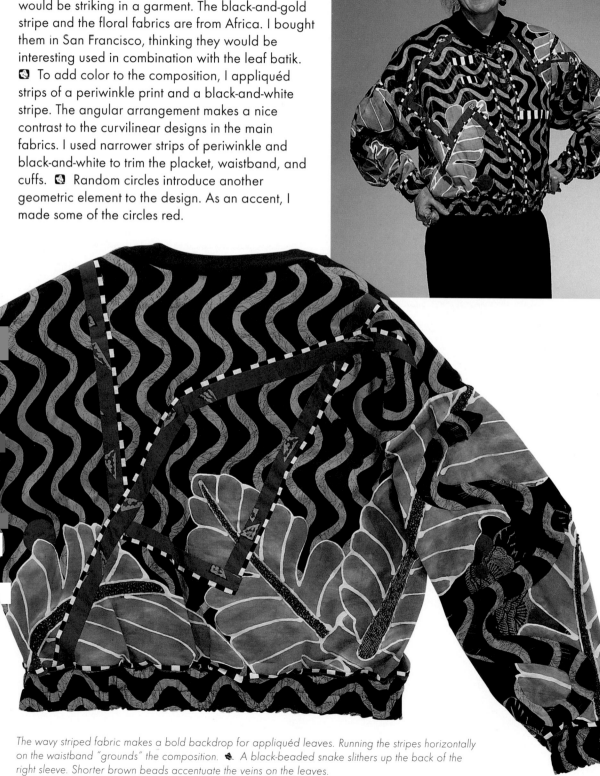

The wavy striped fabric makes a bold backdrop for appliquéd leaves. Running the stripes horizontally on the waistband "grounds" the composition. ❧ A black-beaded snake slithers up the back of the right sleeve. Shorter brown beads accentuate the veins on the leaves.

Silks

For my first contribution to a Fairfield fashion show, I wanted to design and make an outfit that reflected what I did in my quilts. I decided to portray pansies, one of my favorite flowers. ◙ For the blossoms, stems, and leaves, I chose a medley of silks in saturated colors. The main fabric is silk charmeuse. Once again, I used my favorite bomber-style jacket pattern because I knew its flowing lines would translate beautifully into silk. ◙ I designed the jacket much as I would a quilt, treating the front, back, and sleeve pieces as my background fabric. I painted the pansies with acrylic paints, then appliquéd them to the jacket pieces. The pansies are outline quilted and embroidered. To complete the design, I added seed beads.

Silks, 1990. *Like most of my quilts, the inspiration for this design came from the garden.*

Firecracker

To create the jacket front and back, I strip pieced a mix of red, white, and blue fabrics. Using a 9° circle wedge ruler, I cut the pieced fabric into segments, reversed the direction on alternate segments, and joined them. Yellow piping inserted into the seams accentuates and separates the segments. I used the same technique on the sleeves, this time with only two fabrics. ◙ I tied the jacket all over with metallic thread "sparklers" and left the tails dangling. The surface is also heavily embellished with blue and white rhinestones. Large red and white plastic star buttons finish it—with a bang, of course!

Firecracker, 1991. *This jacket was my second Fairfield garment.*

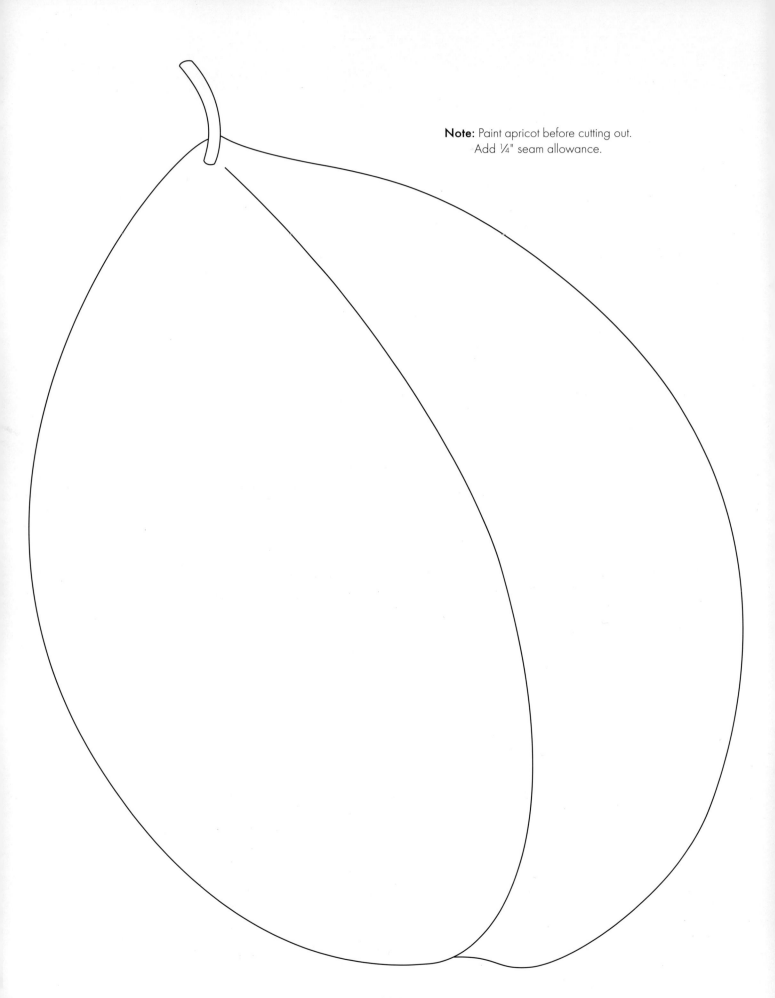

Note: Paint apricot before cutting out.
Add ¼" seam allowance.

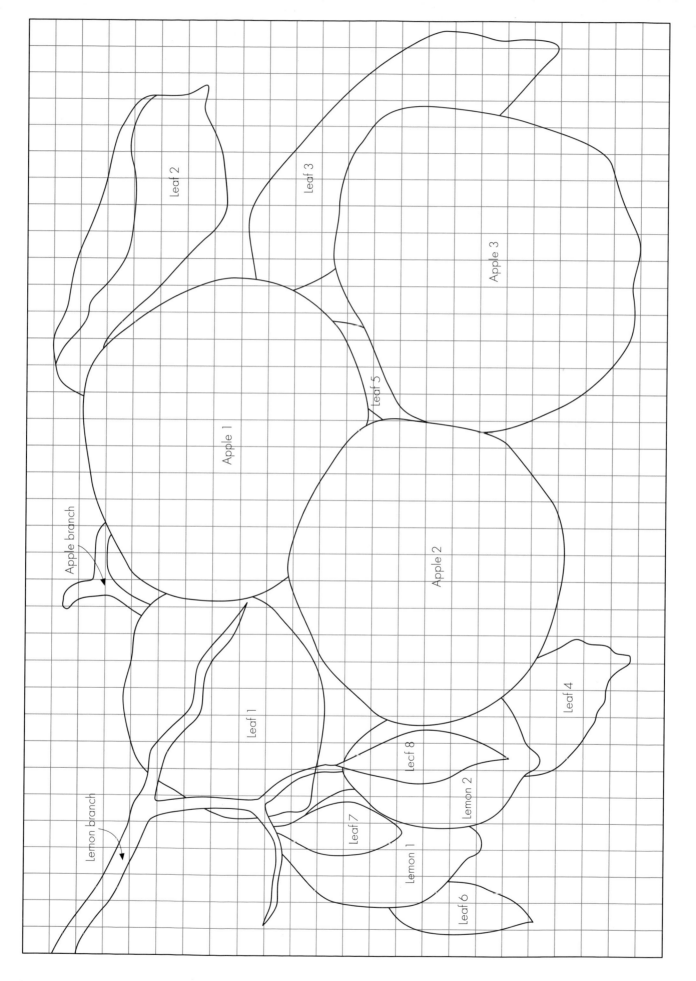

Leaf 2

Leaf 3

Apple 3

Leaf 5

Apple 1

Apple branch

Apple 2

Leaf 1

Leaf 4

Lecf 8

Lemon 2

Lemon branch

Leaf 7

Lemon 1

Leaf 6

Related Titles from
Fiber Studio Press and That Patchwork Place

FIBER STUDIO PRESS

Erika Carter: Personal Imagery in Art Quilts
  • Erika Carter
The Nature of Design
  • Joan Colvin
*Velda Newman: A Painter's Approach
  to Quilt Design*
  • Velda Newman with Christine Barnes

Appliqué in Bloom • Gabrielle Swain
Bargello Quilts • Marge Edie
Blockbender Quilts • Margaret J. Miller
Botanical Wreaths • Laura M. Reinstatler
Colourwash Quilts • Deirdre Amsden
Designing Quilts • Suzanne Hammond
Freedom in Design • Mia Rozmyn
Quilted Sea Tapestries • Ginny Eckley
Quilts from Nature • Joan Colvin
Watercolor Impressions
  • Pat Magaret & Donna Slusser
Watercolor Quilts • Pat Magaret & Donna Slusser

Many titles are available at your local quilt shop or
where fine books are sold. For more information,
send $2 for a color catalog to That Patchwork Place, Inc.,
PO Box 118, Bothell, WA 98041-0118 USA.

U.S. and Canada, call **1-800-426-3126** for the name and
location of the quilt shop nearest you.
Int'l: 1-206-483-3313 **Fax:** 1-206-486-7596
E-mail: info@patchwork.com
Web: http://patchwork.com